Michigan
COOKS' COLLECTION

The American Cancer Society
Michigan Division, Inc.

There is no such thing as a book of entirely new and original recipes and no originality is claimed for the recipes contained in this book. This book represents a collection of favorite recipes submitted by contributors who vouch for their excellence.

Copyright © 1979 by The American Cancer Society, Michigan Division, Inc.

No part of this book may be reproduced or utilized in any form or by any means, electronic or mechanical, including photocopying and recording, or by any information storage and retrieval system, without permission in writing from the publisher.

International Standard Book Number—0-918544-26-2

Printed in the United States of America
WIMMER BROTHERS FINE PRINTING & LITHOGRAPHY
Memphis, Tennessee 38118

"Cookbooks of Distinction"™

IN APPRECIATION

We wish to express our deepest appreciation to the following companies who have provided funding to support this project. They are listed in alphabetical order:

Chelsea Milling Company, Chelsea, Michigan
Hiram Walker, Inc., Detroit, Michigan
Vlasic Foods, Inc., W. Bloomfield, Michigan
Whirlpool Corporation, Benton Harbor, Michigan

Because of their generosity, almost all of the proceeds of the sale of these books will be able to be applied toward the American Cancer Society's programs of research, education and service to the cancer patient.

FOREWORD

Michigan Cooks' Collection has been published as a fund-raising project for the Michigan Division of the American Cancer Society. It is the product of the efforts of many dedicated volunteers who were kind enough to share their favorite recipes.

Our thanks to the County Units who have devoted their time and efforts to this worthwhile project. A special thanks also to the Michigan Division staff for their support in the organization and coordination of the project.

To those of you making a donation toward this cookbook we say 'thanks', knowing that by your contribution, you have helped bring the day of 'Freedom from Cancer' closer to being a reality.

We wish you many hours of enjoyment and pleasure in using the Michigan Cooks' Collection.

Marilyn Turner
Cookbook Chairperson

Rusty Staub
Honorary Chairman

Fred Graczyk
Restaurant Chairman

Richard H. White
Michigan Division
Crusade Committee Chairman

TABLE OF CONTENTS

Appetizers 7
Soups, Salads and Sandwiches 19
Breads 31
Vegetables 43
Fish and Poultry 53
Entrees 65
International Collection 81
Desserts 99
Michigan Fruit Basket 139
Microwave 157
Michigan Restaurant Sampler 167
Index 185

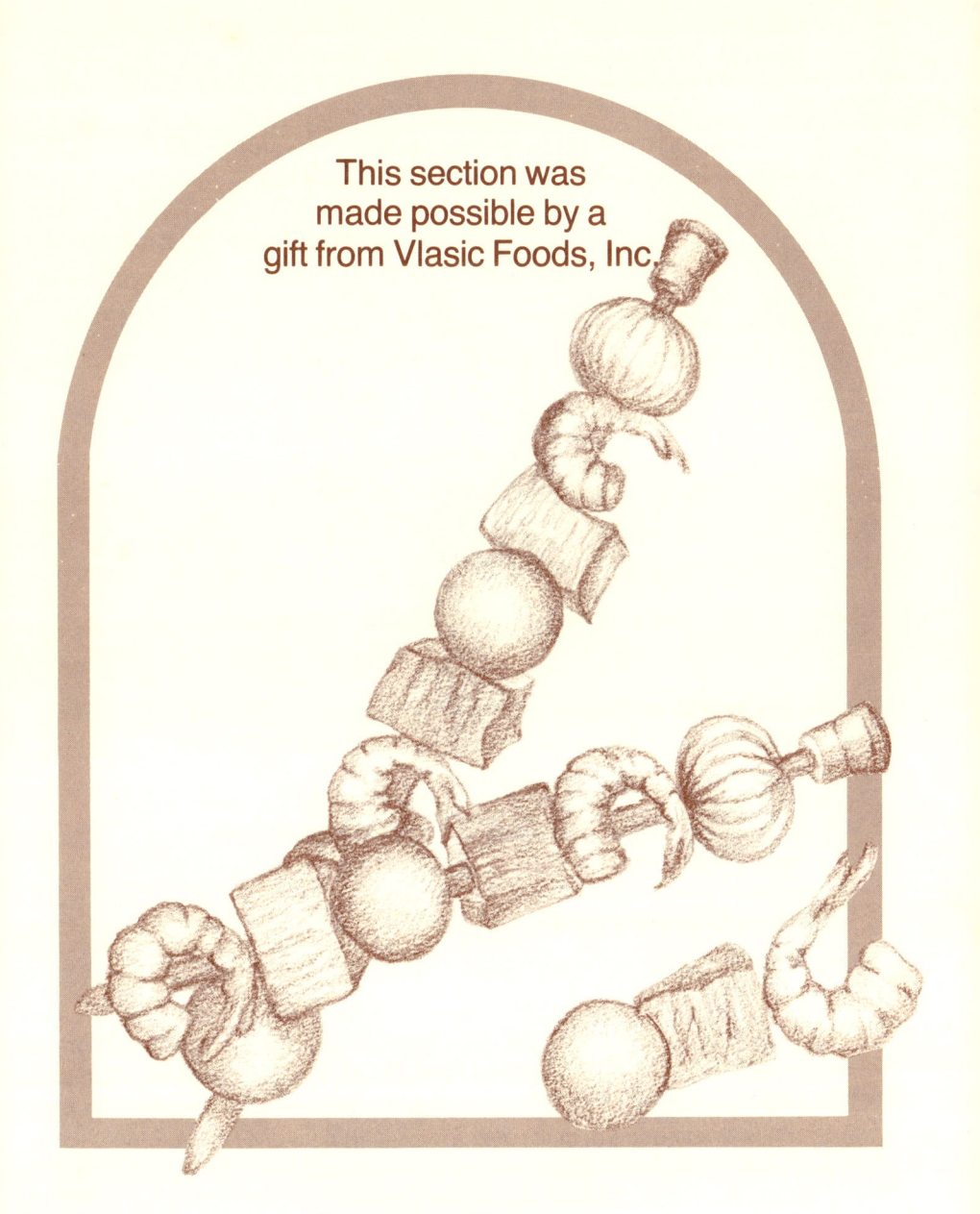

This section was
made possible by a
gift from Vlasic Foods, Inc.

Appetizers

Appetizers

PIZZA PICKLES

Vlasic Dill Chips, well
   drained on paper towels
Pepperoni sausage, sliced

Mozzarella cheese, sliced
Ritz crackers

Stack Vlasic Dill Chip, pepperoni sausage and Mozzarella cheese on a Ritz cracker. Place under broiler just until cheese bubbles.

Nancy Vlasic
Oakland County (Bloomfield Hills)

PARTY CHEESE BAKE

4 cups saltine crackers, crushed
1 cup butter, melted
½ teaspoon curry powder
2 cups sweet onion, chopped medium fine and lightly salted
1½ cups Cheddar cheese, grated

3 cups milk, scalded
3 eggs, lightly beaten
1 teaspoon salt
Dash of red pepper
Parmesan cheese
Paprika

Coat crushed cracker crumbs with mixture of melted butter and curry powder. Line an 11x16-inch pan with ¾ of cracker mixture. Spread chopped onion over crackers and cover with Cheddar cheese. Combine scalded milk with eggs, salt and pepper. Pour over ingredients in pan. Sprinkle on balance of crackers. Top with light layer of Parmesan cheese and paprika. Bake at 375 degrees for 25 minutes. Cut into 2-inch squares. Serves 40. *Note: This is much tastier when served warm. A sprig of parsley adds a festive touch!*

Mrs. Alfred Lape (Helen)
Kalkaska County (Fife Lake)

CHEESE DELIGHTS

Appetizers

12 slices white bread
2 sticks butter or margarine
2 cups cottage cheese
½ cup Romano cheese, grated
3 eggs
1 cup Philadelphia cream cheese

Cut corners off of bread. Take each slice of bread and roll thin with rolling pin. Melt your 2 sticks of butter or margarine and dip each slice of bread into the butter. Put each slice of bread in a 12 cup cake tin. Mold them with your hands. Cream cottage and Philadelphia cream, and Romano cheese with eggs. Fill each cup cake tin about ¾ full. Preheat oven to 375 degrees. Bake your Cheese Delights for about 25 to 30 minutes, or until golden brown. Serve hot. *Note: If you have any filling left, just take more bread and fill another cup cake tin with the left-over filling.*

Marina Chapekis
Delta County (Escanaba)

. . . To slice cheese thinly, heat knife first.

MOTHER REVZIN'S MEATBALLS

2 pounds ground beef
1 bottle chili sauce and 1 equal bottle water
2 bay leaves
1 tablespoon lemon juice
¼ cup and 1 tablespoon brown sugar, packed
1½ cups pineapple chunks

Form ground beef into tiny meatballs. Place in a pot and add chili sauce, water, bay leaves, lemon juice and brown sugar. Simmer on top of stove, covered for ½ hour. Add pineapple chunks. Cook an additional 1½ hours or until done. Serves 12 as an appetizer in a chafing dish or 6 to 8 as a main course.

Naomi Revzin
Ingham County (East Lansing)

Appetizers

COCKTAIL MEATBALLS

2 cups fresh bread cubes
½ cup milk
1½ pounds ground beef
1 can water chestnuts, finely chopped
½ teaspoon onion powder
1 teaspoon soy sauce
½ teaspoon Tabasco sauce
½ teaspoon Accent
1 teaspoon garlic salt

Soak bread in milk and squeeze dry. Mix together ground beef, water chestnuts, onion powder, soy sauce, Tabasco sauce, Accent and garlic salt. Form mixture into small balls and brown on cookie sheet in oven. Drain off excess fat. Add meatballs to sauce and serve in chafing dish. Makes approximately 100 small balls.

Sauce:
2 cups brown sugar
2 teaspoons dry mustard
1 cup wine vinegar
1 cup water

Combine all sauce ingredients in saucepan and simmer until sugar is dissolved. Add meatballs to sauce and serve in chafing dish.

Mrs. Alexander Brede, III
Ingham County (East Lansing)

HOLIDAY MEATBALLS

Meatballs:
1 pound ground beef
1 cup bread crumbs
1 egg
⅓ cup onion, minced
1 tablespoon snipped parsley
¼ cup milk
1 teaspoon salt
⅛ teaspoon pepper
½ teaspoon Worcestershire sauce

Combine all meatball ingredients together. Mix thoroughly; divide and shape into bite-size meatballs. Brown gently in oil until cooked through. Heat sauce in fondue or saucepan and add meatballs. Simmer slowly for 30 minutes. Serve.

Sauce:
1 12-ounce jar chili sauce
1 10-ounce jar grape jelly

Combine chili sauce and grape jelly in saucepan or fondue. Heat through and add meatballs.

Mrs. H. C. Havlik (Rose)
Shiawassee County (Owosso)

MAGIC MEATBALLS

1 pound ground beef
2 cups small bread pieces
  (about 2 slices)

1 package onion soup mix
1 egg, slightly beaten
1 tablespoon dry parsley leaves

Preheat oven to 350 degrees. In large mixing bowl, add ground beef, bread crumbs, onion soup mix, egg and dry parsley leaves. Mix well and form into small meatballs by rolling in hands. Size of meatballs depends on your personal preference. Place meatballs in rows in a glass baking dish. Pour Magic Sauce over meatballs and cook for 45 minutes at 350 degrees. *Note: Meatballs may be made ahead of time and frozen, but do not freeze sauce.*

Magic Sauce:
1 cup catsup
⅓ cup Real Lemon juice

⅓ cup grape jelly

Combine ingredients thoroughly and pour over meatballs.

Linda Marie Beehler
Kalkaska County (Kalkaska)

. . . Dip your fingers in water before rolling meatballs, it prevents sticking.

CORNED BEEF ROLLS

1 12-ounce can corned beef
½ pint sour cream
½ envelope Lipton onion soup
  mix

2 dozen small white rolls

Mix corned beef, sour cream and onion soup mix together thoroughly. Spread mixture on rolls. Place rolls on baking sheet, cover with foil and bake at 350 degrees for 30 minutes. Serve immediately. *Note: Mixture may be made ahead of time and stored in refrigerator. May also be prepared on larger buns such as hamburger buns and served as a sandwich.*

Mrs. Richard W. Lamkin (Gloria)
Kent County (Grand Rapids)

Appetizers

BOURBON COCKTAIL HOT DOGS

1 pound hot dogs, cut into bite-sized pieces
¾ cup bourbon
½ cup catsup
½ cup brown sugar
1 tablespoon onion, grated

Blend bourbon, catsup, brown sugar and onion in saucepan. Bring to boil and add hot dogs. Simmer hot dogs in sauce for 1 hour. Serve in chafing dish. *Note: This recipe can be made a day or 2 ahead. Store in refrigerator. Remove and heat 1 hour before serving.*

Kathryn M. Csont
Wayne County (Trenton)

HOLIDAY APPETIZER PIE

1 8-ounce package cream cheese
2 tablespoons milk
1 2½-ounce jar dried beef, snipped
2 tablespoons instant minced onion
2 tablespoons green pepper, chopped
⅛ teaspoon pepper
½ cup dairy sour cream
¼ cup walnuts, chopped

Blend cheese and milk. Stir in dried beef, onion, green pepper and pepper. Mix well and stir in sour cream. Place in an 8-inch pie plate or shallow baking dish. Sprinkle walnuts on top and bake in preheated 350 degree oven for 15 minutes. Serve with assorted crackers.

Mrs. Darryl Rogers (Marsha)
Ingham County (East Lansing)

RAW VEGETABLE DIP

⅔ cup sour cream
⅔ cup Hellman's mayonnaise
1 tablespoon onion, minced
1 tablespoon parsley flakes
1 teaspoon dill weed
1 teaspoon seasoned salt

Mix together sour cream and mayonnaise. Add minced onion, parsley flakes, dill weed and seasoned salt. Mix well and serve with raw vegetables.

Debbie Baugh
Kalkaska County (Kalkaska)

VEGETABLE DIP

⅔ cup Hellman's mayonnaise
⅔ cup sour cream
1 tablespoon dry onion
1 tablespoon dry parsley
2 drops Tabasco

1 teaspoon Worcestershire sauce
1 teaspoon seasoned salt
½ teaspoon Accent
1 teaspoon dill seed or weed

Combine all ingredients and refrigerate. *Note: Use as a fresh vegetable dip for celery, carrot sticks, cauliflower, green pepper, etc.*

Mary Anne Rankin
Calhoun County (Battle Creek)

FRESH VEGETABLE DIP

1 8-ounce package cream cheese
⅓ cup Del Monte chili sauce
¼ cup lemon juice
1 tablespoon Wright's liquid smoke

1 tablespoon Worcestershire sauce
½ teaspoon garlic salt (Optional)
½ teaspoon onion salt (Optional)

Place all ingredients in mixing bowl and beat with electric beater slowly until thoroughly mixed. Serve with fresh vegetables. May be made a day ahead or just before serving. Keeps in refrigerator for several days.

Mrs. John Orr (Romie)
Washtenaw County (Ann Arbor)

GUACAMOLE WITH WINTER VEGETABLES

2 medium-size ripe avocados
1 cup tomato, peeled and diced
1 tablespoon onion, finely chopped
¼ cup French Dressing

1 teaspoon canned hot chilies, finely chopped
Dash Tabasco sauce
1 tablespoon lemon or lime juice
Salt and pepper to taste

Peel and mash the 2 avocados. Add all other ingredients and mix well. Press plastic wrap closely over surface of guacamole to prevent it from darkening. Chill until served. *Note: Delicious served with carrot sticks, cauliflowerettes, cucumber sticks, cherry tomatoes and radishes.*

Marilyn Danko, Cooking Instructor
Oakland County (Royal Oak)

Appetizers

PEANUT BUTTER PATÉ

1 4-ounce can mushrooms, drained and chopped
2 tablespoons butter
2 tablespoons lemon juice
1 8-ounce package cream cheese, softened
2 tablespoons smooth peanut butter
2 slices bacon, fried and crumbled

In small skillet, sauté mushrooms in butter for 2 minutes. Stir in lemon juice. In medium bowl beat cream cheese and peanut butter until fluffy. Add mushroom mixture and bacon. Stir well. Cover and refrigerate at least 1 hour. Serve with crackers or celery sticks. Yield: About 1½ cups.

Mrs. Gerald W. Zinger (Anita)
Wayne County (Dearborn)

GALA PECAN SPREAD

8 ounces cream cheese
2 tablespoons milk
5 ounces smoked beef
2 tablespoons dry onion flakes
¼ cup green pepper
½ teaspoon garlic salt
½ cup sour cream
2 tablespoons butter
½ teaspoon salt
½ cup pecans, chopped

Soften cream cheese and blend with milk. Cut beef finely and blend into cheese with green pepper, onion flakes and garlic. Fold in sour cream. Spoon into an 8-inch pie plate, melt butter, add salt and pecans. Bake at 350 degrees for 20 minutes. Serve hot on crackers. *Note: Can be made ahead and put in freezer.*

Mrs. Robert Pfeuffer (Ellen)
Kalkaska County (Kalkaska)

LIVER PASTE

1 pound chicken livers
3 tablespoons onion, chopped
½ teaspoon salt
¼ teaspoon dry mustard
¼ teaspoon pepper
6 tablespoons margarine or butter, softened

Sauté chicken livers and onions until done, but not browned. Cool slightly. Puree 1 cup at a time in blender. Stir in salt, dry mustard, pepper and margarine or butter. Refrigerate.

Evelyn Hartwick
Bay County (Pinconning)

SUPER GREAT CRAB SPREAD

½ large onion, grated and juice
12 ounces cream cheese
2 teaspoons Worcestershire sauce
Garlic salt to taste
1 tablespoon lemon juice
2 tablespoons mayonnaise
9 ounces seafood cocktail sauce
¾ pound crabmeat, cooked
Parsley

Grate onion in mixing bowl. Add cream cheese, Worcestershire sauce, garlic salt, lemon juice and mayonnaise. Cream well and spread over large plate or platter. Cover with cocktail sauce and then crabmeat. Dried parsley may be sprinkled on top. Refrigerate overnight and serve with crackers. *Note: I use 1 7-ounce package frozen crab that is well-drained and 1 small can crab. You may try tuna or chicken instead of crab.*

Mrs. Richard Peters (Nancy)
Muskegon County (Muskegon)

HOT CRABMEAT SPREAD

1 8-ounce package cream cheese
1 tablespoon coffee cream
1 7-ounce can crabmeat
1 teaspoon horseradish
2 tablespoons onion, grated
Salt to taste
½ cup slivered or sliced almonds

Combine cream cheese, coffee cream, crabmeat, horseradish, onion, salt and almonds. Place mixture in small oven-proof casserole dish. Bake at 375 degrees for 20 minutes or until bubbly. Serve with Ritz-type crackers or party rye bread.

Mrs. Irwin Deutch (Lynne)
Oakland County (Birmingham)

SHRIMP SPREAD

1½ packages Knox gelatin
½ cup cold water
1 can tomato soup, undiluted
1 8-ounce package Philadelphia cream cheese
1 cup Miracle Whip
1 cup onion, chopped
1 cup celery, chopped
2 4⅓-ounce cans shrimp, drained

Soften Knox gelatin in cold water. Heat the tomato soup, adding chunks of Philadelphia cream cheese until all is melted. Remove from heat. Add Miracle Whip and Knox gelatin to soup mixture. Beat until smooth and add onion, celery, and shrimp. Pour into greased mold and chill in refrigerator 24 hours. Serves 15. *Note: Greased oleo tubs work very well. This spread can be prepared ahead of time and frozen.*

Mrs. Eric Bailey (Carol)
Gratiot County (St. Louis)

Appetizers

Appetizers

PICKLED BEETS AND EGGS

8 medium beets or 1 29-ounce can sliced beets
12 hard-boiled eggs, shells removed
1 teaspoon salt
1 teaspoon sugar
1 teaspoon mustard
1 cup water
1 cup vinegar

Cook beets until tender. Blanch, skin and slice. Bring to a boil salt, sugar, mustard, vinegar and water. Pack eggs and beets alternately in a 2-quart jar or bowl. Cover with hot juice and refrigerate overnight, covered.

Mrs. Herbert Hertzler (Helen)
Iosco County (East Tawas)

TWENTY FOUR HOUR BROCCOLI

2 to 3 bunches broccoli
1 cup cider vinegar
1½ cups Wesson oil
1 tablespoon sugar
1 tablespoon dill weed
1 tablespoon Accent
1 teaspoon salt
1 teaspoon pepper
1 teaspoon garlic salt

Clean, rinse and cut up broccoli into 1 to 2-inch pieces. In a large bowl mix together vinegar, oil, sugar, dill weed, Accent, salt, pepper and garlic salt. Add broccoli to mixture and stir until broccoli is well coated. Cover and put in refrigerator for 24 hours. Drain liquid off and serve.

Mrs. Ron Schrage (Judy)
Emmet County (Petoskey)

CARROT RELISH

6 cups carrots, sliced
¼ cup water
1 cup sugar
1 teaspoon salt
½ teaspoon pepper (Optional)
1 10¾-ounce can tomato soup
1 cup vegetable oil
¾ cup cider vinegar
1 cup onion, diced
1 cup green pepper, diced
1 clove garlic, minced (Optional)

Cook carrots in water until tender; drain. Mix sugar, salt and pepper together and add tomato soup, oil and vinegar. Mix well. Add cooked carrots, onion, green pepper and garlic. Mix well and place in 1-quart jar. Cover and marinate overnight. Serve as a relish or over lettuce. *Note: Keeps in refrigerator for 3 to 4 weeks.*

Mrs. Donovan D. Wharff (Josephine)
Oakland County (Rochester)

CARROTS SUPREME

4 pounds carrots, peeled and
   sliced crosswise
2 onions, sliced
1 green pepper, sliced
1 tablespoon salt
1 teaspoon dried mustard
½ teaspoon pepper
1 cup sugar
1 cup oil
¾ cup vinegar
1 can tomato soup

Boil carrots until easily pierced with a fork. Place carrots, onions, and green pepper in large bowl. Combine salt, mustard, pepper, sugar, oil, vinegar and tomato soup in blender and mix thoroughly. Pour vinegar mixture over vegetables. Cover and marinate in refrigerator overnight.

Gretchen Crawford
Osceola County (Reed City)

... Freshen vegetables by soaking them in cold water with a little lemon juice.

CRISP MARINATED CARROTS AND VEGETABLES

2 1-pound packages carrots
   (approximately 5 cups)
1 cup sugar
½ cup salad oil
½ cup cider vinegar
½ teaspoon salt
¼ teaspoon celery seed
4 stalks celery, sliced
1 medium onion, sliced
1 sweet green pepper, cut into
   strips

Cut carrots into discs. Cook in salted water until crisp tender only. Mix in separate bowl the sugar, oil, vinegar, salt and celery seed. Drain carrots and place in large mixing bowl. Add liquid ingredients and mix. Add celery, onion and pepper and mix well. Refrigerate and serve after aging and completely chilling. Will keep in refrigerator for several weeks and flavor improves with aging. Drain liquid and serve as salad or cold vegetable dish. *Note: Green onion or scallion rings may be substituted for onion slices.*

Mrs. Myles Musgrave (Elizabeth)
St. Clair County (Port Huron)

Appetizers

MARINATED CARROTS

2 pounds carrots
1 large onion, sliced in rings
1 large green pepper, sliced in strips
1 cup sugar
½ cup vegetable oil
½ cup vinegar
1 teaspoon dry mustard
1 teaspoon Worcestershire sauce
1 can tomato soup, undiluted

Cut carrots into 2-inch sticks. Boil in small amount of water until just tender. Do not overcook. Cool. Slice onion into thin rings. Slice green pepper into thin strips. Combine sugar, vegetable oil, vinegar, dry mustard, Worcestershire sauce and tomato soup. Mix thoroughly. Pour over cooled carrots, onion and green pepper. Marinate at room temperature for 4 hours. Pour into jars and refrigerate. Good for several weeks.

Gloria Nikkari
Gratiot County (St. Louis)

. . . To make pretty carrot curls, slice a carrot very thinly lengthwise. Drop in ice water. The curl is natural and permanent.

GREEN TOMATO MINCEMEAT

1 peck green tomatoes, chopped
1 peck apples, chopped
3 pounds raisins
2 cups water
2 cups vinegar
5 pounds brown sugar
2 cups suet
3 tablespoons allspice
3 tablespoons cinnamon
1 tablespoon cloves

Pour boiling water over chopped green tomatoes 3 times and drain. Mix all ingredients together in large canning kettle. Cook until tender. Pack in hot jars and seal. Yield: 8 quarts.

Jeano Hoffrichter
Oakland County (Milford)

Soups, Salads and Sandwiches

TOULA'S CREAM OF ASPARAGUS SOUP

3 shallots, chopped
1 stick butter
3 tablespoons flour
2 cups chicken broth
1 teaspoon salt
Pinch of white pepper
1 pound fresh asparagus, cleaned and chopped
½ cup heavy cream
2 egg yolks

Sauté shallots in hot butter until transparent. Add flour and stir until well combined. Turn heat on high and add chicken broth, lemon juice, salt and pepper. Bring to a rolling boil. Add chopped asparagus and turn heat to low. Simmer for 20 minutes. In a food processor or blender, puree soup until smooth. Return to soup pot. Mix ½ cup heavy cream and 2 egg yolks in a cup. Reheat the soup and gradually add the cream-egg mixture. Serve immediately.

Toula Patsalis
Kitchen Glamor Stores
Wayne County (Redford)

ITALIAN GARDEN SOUP

1 large onion, chopped
1 large clove garlic, crushed
2 tablespoons butter or margarine
2 13-ounce cans chicken broth
1 16-ounce can tomatoes
1 16-ounce can green beans
1 zucchini, sliced in big chunks
1½ cups carrots, thinly sliced
1½ cups celery, sliced
1 teaspoon each of salt and oregano
¼ teaspoon basil
⅛ teaspoon pepper

In large kettle or Dutch oven, sauté onion and garlic in butter about 15 minutes. Add chicken broth, vegetables, salt, oregano, basil and pepper; cover and simmer 1 hour or until vegetables are tender crisp. Serve in soup bowls topped with croutons or grated Parmesan cheese if desired. *Note:* Left-over chicken or turkey may be added or if you prefer a different vegetable, one may be substituted for any of the above vegetables. Example–1 can corn or 1 can diced potatoes would be a nice change.

Mrs. Paul Gravenstreter (Pat)
Oakland County (Farmington)

MINESTRONE

¼ cup Wesson oil
1 clove garlic, minced
1 cup onion, chopped
1 cup celery, chopped
2 6-ounce cans tomato paste
1 10½-ounce can beef broth
2½ quarts water
1 cup cabbage, chopped
1 10-ounce package frozen peas and carrots
2½ teaspoons salt
¼ teaspoon pepper
½ teaspoon rosemary leaves
1 can kidney beans, undrained
1 cup elbow macaroni
Parmesan cheese

Heat oil in large kettle and sauté garlic, onion and celery for 5 minutes. Stir in tomato paste, beef broth, water, cabbage, peas and carrots, salt, pepper and rosemary leaves. Bring to boil, cover and simmer slowly for 1 hour. Add kidney beans and elbow macaroni. Cook 15 minutes longer. Garnish with Parmesan cheese. Serves 6 to 8. *Note: Leftovers keep well in refrigerator or freezer.*

Mrs. James F. Nowicki
Macomb County (Mt. Clemens)

BEEF STEW

1 pint tomatoes
1 cup celery
4 carrots
4 onions
6 or 7 potatoes
1½ pounds stew meat
3 tablespoons Tapioca
1 tablespoon sugar
1 teaspoon salt

Cut up vegetables. Place all ingredients in large glass baking dish. Cover with foil and bake at 250 degrees for 5 hours.

Mrs. Dennis Emery (Sharon)
Lapeer County (Metamora)

CAROLINA COLE SLAW

1 cup white sugar
1 teaspoon salt
1 teaspoon dry mustard
1 teaspoon celery seed
1 cup vinegar
⅔ cup vegetable or corn oil
1 large cabbage, shredded
1 medium green pepper, diced
1 medium sweet onion, diced

Combine sugar, salt, mustard, celery seed, vinegar and oil. Bring to a boil. Cool thoroughly and pour over vegetables. Mix well. *Note: This will keep in refrigerator for 2 weeks.*

Mary Davisson
Oscoda County (Mio)

Salads

GERMAN POTATO SALAD

5 slices bacon, diced
½ cup onion, diced
3 tablespoons flour
1 cup hot water

⅔ cup sugar
1 teaspoon salt
½ cup vinegar
8 potatoes, cooked with skins on

Dice bacon and fry. Remove bacon from pan and fry onions in bacon grease until transparent, but not brown. Remove onions. To grease in pan, add flour, blending well and adding hot water to make a medium thick sauce. Add sugar, salt and vinegar and return bacon and onions to sauce and mix. Peel and slice warm potatoes being careful not to smash potato slices. Bake at 350 degrees for 1 hour and serve hot. Serves 8 to 10.

Mrs. Kenneth W. Peterson
Menominee County (Daggett)

HOT POTATO SALAD

8 cans round sliced potatoes
16 to 20 ounces Cheddar cheese, grated
1 to 1½ cups mayonnaise or salad dressing

½ cup green olives, sliced
½ cup bacon, chopped
Salt and pepper to taste

Toss together all of the above ingredients. Place in greased 3-quart casserole dish and bake at 325 degrees for 1 hour.

Kathleen C. Hasse
Oakland County (Farmington)

24 HOUR CABBAGE SLAW

1 cup sugar
½ cup salad oil
1 cup vinegar
½ cup water
¼ teaspoon salt

¼ teaspoon garlic salt
1 medium head cabbage
1 small onion, chopped (or onion salt)

Combine sugar, oil, vinegar, water, salt and garlic salt and mix well. Pour over cabbage and onion several hours before eating. This improves with age and will keep very well for many days. *Note: I like to chop my vegetables in the blender with water and drain in a colander. When I do this I omit the water called for in the dressing. For our family of 5, I use half of all the dressing ingredients and still have enough for 2 meals.*

Mrs. James Toth (Sue)
Cass County (Edwardsburg)

TOMATO SHRIMP SALAD

1 10¾-ounce can tomato soup
½ cup water
1 envelope unflavored gelatin softened with ¼ cup cold water
1 cup mayonnaise
1 8-ounce package cream cheese
½ cup celery, chopped
½ cup onion, chopped
½ cup green pepper, chopped
1 6-ounce bag precooked frozen shrimp, thawed, chopped, and drained

Dilute tomato soup with water. Heat to boiling and add softened gelatin and cool. Beat together mayonnaise and cream cheese. Add soup mixture slowly. Stir in celery, green pepper, onion, and shrimp. Grease an 8-cup mold with oil. Pour in salad mixture and chill until firm. Garnish with lettuce leaves and black olives. Serves 8.

Andrea Smith
Ingham County (Okemos)

. . . If crackers lose their crispness heat in a slow oven and when cool, they will be crisp again.

SPINACH SALAD

1 pound fresh spinach
1 egg
1 tablespoon Parmesan cheese, grated
1 clove garlic, minced
1½ teaspoons Dijon mustard
½ teaspoon salt
Freshly ground pepper
3 tablespoons lemon juice
½ cup salad oil
Sesame seeds, toasted or plain (Optional)

In a large basin of cold water, thoroughly but quickly wash 1 pound of fresh spinach. Remove stems and break large pieces into smaller ones. Make dressing by mixing all ingredients except sesame seeds in a jar and shake thoroughly. *Note: You may put dressing ingredients in a blender and blend until thoroughly homogenized.*

Rana Schwartz
Kent County (Grand Rapids)

SPINACH SALAD WITH DRESSING

1 pound bag fresh spinach
½ pound bacon, cooked and crumbled
1 can water chestnuts, sliced
4 hard-boiled eggs, chopped
1 cup fresh mushrooms, sliced
1 avocado, sliced (Optional)

Combine all ingredients in salad bowl. Top with dressing and toss.

Dressing:
⅓ cup sugar
1 tablespoon Worcestershire sauce
1 cup olive oil
1 onion, chopped
⅓ cup catsup
1 teaspoon salt
¼ cup red wine vinegar

Place all ingredients in blender and blend until smooth. Pour over spinach salad.

Mary Cheek
Tuscola County (Vassar)

. . . Sprinkle grated lemon peel over a salad to perk it up.

LAYERED GREEN SALAD

1 head lettuce, cut up
½ cup celery, chopped
½ cup green onions, chopped
½ cup green pepper, chopped
½ cup carrots, grated
1 10-ounce package frozen peas
1 pint Hellmans mayonnaise
2 tablespoons sugar
8 ounces Cheddar cheese, grated
10 strips bacon, diced and fried crisp

Place lettuce in bottom of large casserole or 9x13-inch pan. Layer the celery, onions, pepper, carrots, frozen peas, mayonnaise and sugar over lettuce. Top with grated cheese and bacon. Cover and refrigerate for at least 8 hours before serving. *Note: Do not cook peas.*

Mrs. Norbert Hanson
Menominee County (Wallace)

Salads

24 HOUR SALAD

2 cups pineapple chunks
2 cups red grapes, seeded
4 cups small marshmallows,
   cut in half

1 cup nuts, chopped

Mix together pineapple, seeded grapes cut in half, marshmallows, and nuts.

Dressing:
4 egg yolks
1¼ cup cream
Juice of 1 lemon

1 teaspoon salt
1 tablespoon sugar
½ pint whipping cream

Cook egg yolks, cream, lemon juice, salt and sugar to a thick consistency. Cool. Add mixture to ½ pint whipping cream. Fold together with fruit mixture and let stand 24 hours before serving.

Mabel V. Kies
Kalkaska County (Kalkaska)

APRICOT CREAM CHEESE DELIGHT

1 6-ounce package apricot
   gelatin
1 No. 2 can crushed pineapple,
   undrained
½ cup sugar
1 cup apricot puree or 2 small
   jars baby food apricots

1 8-ounce package cream cheese,
   softened
1 large can evaporated milk,
   chilled
⅔ cup nuts, chopped

Combine gelatin and pineapple, heat until mixture simmers. Add sugar, apricot puree and softened cream cheese. Continue heating until cheese melts. I usually beat with mixer to break it up. Remove from heat and chill until mixture mounds. Whip evaporated milk until peaks form. Fold in apricot mixture. Pour into 9x13-inch cake pan. Top with chopped nuts. Serves 15 or more.

Helen Knowles
Gratiot County (St. Louis)

Salads

CHERRY-PINEAPPLE SALAD

1 3-ounce package lemon Jello
2 cups boiling water
1½ cups miniature marshmallows
2 small packages Philadelphia cream cheese, softened

1 No. 2 can crushed pineapple, drained
1 cup pineapple juice
½ pint whipping cream
1 3-ounce package cherry Jello
1 cup boiling water

Dissolve lemon Jello in 2 cups boiling water. Add marshmallows. Stir until melted. Add softened cream cheese. Beat until smooth and let set until partially thickened. Add drained pineapple. Fold in whipped cream. Chill in a 2-quart baking dish until firm. Dissolve cherry Jello in 1 cup boiling water. Add 1 cup pineapple juice and let cool to room temperature. Pour over bottom layer and let set until firm.

Elaine Skory
Manistee County (Manistee)

. . . Line your congealed salad molds with salad oil and the finished salad will slide out easily.

FROZEN SALAD

1 3-ounce package cream cheese
1 4-ounce bottle maraschino cherries, reserve juice
⅓ cup mayonnaise
½ cup crushed pineapple, drained

2 medium oranges, diced or 1 can mandarin oranges, drained
1 cup Cool Whip
2 tablespoons sugar
½ cup pecans, chopped

Soften cheese and add liquid from cherries; add mayonnaise and blend. Cut cherries into small pieces; add pineapple and oranges. Whip cream, fold in sugar, fruits and nuts. Chill or freeze.

Mrs. Donald Gillette (Marjorie)
Cass County (Niles)

RIBBON SALAD

First Layer:
2 packages unflavored gelatin
¾ cup cold water
2 cups milk
1 cup white sugar
1 teaspoon vanilla
2 cups sour cream

Dissolve unflavored gelatin in ¾ cup cold water and set aside. Combine milk and sugar and heat until steaming. Remove from heat and add gelatin mixture. Stir until dissolved and cool 10 minutes. Add sour cream and vanilla and stir until well blended.

Second Layer:
1 3-ounce package each: *
  Orange gelatin
  Lemon gelatin
  Lime gelatin
For each package of gelatin:
  ¾ cup hot water
  ¾ cup cold water

*Any combination of gelatin may be used.

Dissolve each package of gelatin separately in hot water; add cold water. Cool slightly.

To Layer:
Pour 1 cup gelatin in 9x9-inch pan. Chill quickly until set. When set, carefully add 1 cup of unflavored gelatin mixture, chill quickly and continue layering until all layers are made. Chill 2 hours before serving.

Jeanine Clemens
Ogemaw County (West Branch)

RHUBARB/STRAWBERRY JELLO

1 cup water
2 cups red rhubarb, finely chopped
1 cup sugar
1 3-ounce box strawberry Jello

Add water to the 2 cups of rhubarb. Cook until tender; blend in sugar and then add Jello. Stir until well mixed. Pour to cool in 4½-ounce glasses. Chill until set. Yield: about 5 glasses. *Note: Very nice to go with Thanksgiving Dinner. Red rhubarb preferred.*

Frances Rifenberg
St. Joseph County (Constantine)

Salads

STRAWBERRY SALAD

1 10-ounce package frozen strawberries
2 cups boiling water
1 6-ounce package strawberry Jello

1 1-pound can crushed pineapple
2 large ripe bananas, mashed
1 1-pound carton sour cream

Thaw frozen berries. Dissolve Jello in boiling water. Add thawed berries with juice and undrained pineapple. Mash and whip bananas and add to Jello mixture. Pour half of mixture into 13x9-inch dish and chill until firm. Spread sour cream over congealed layer and carefully cover with remaining Jello mixture. Chill until firm. Serves 12 to 16.

Mrs. Donald Wood (Ellen)
Kalkaska County (Kalkaska)

BLUE CHEESE DRESSING

1 4-ounce package crumbled blue cheese
⅛ teaspoon garlic salt

1 cup sour cream
1 cup mayonnaise

Mix all ingredients very well and put in covered jar. Let set for a day before using. Good for salads or dips or on baked potatoes. Must be refrigerated. *Note: Keeps 1 week.*

Mrs. Timothy Achterhoff (Mary)
Muskegon County (North Muskegon)

CELERY SEED DRESSING

⅔ cup granulated sugar
½ teaspoon dry mustard
1 teaspoon salt
1 small onion, peeled and cut

1 cup salad oil
½ cup vinegar
1 tablespoon celery seed
Few drops yellow food coloring

Combine all ingredients in a blender and blend until thoroughly mixed. This is an excellent basic sweet/sour dressing and keeps well in refrigerator.

Catherine VandeBunte
Kalamazoo County (Augusta)

EASY CAESAR SALAD DRESSING

1 egg
2 cloves garlic, crushed
½ cup Wesson oil
⅛ teaspoon red or cayenne pepper
¼ teaspoon salt
1 tablespoon vinegar
½ cup Parmesan cheese, grated
¾ cup croutons

Beat egg with garlic. Add oil, red pepper, salt and vinegar. Beat again. Add Parmesan cheese last and beat until blended. Pour over broken salad greens, add croutons and toss. *Note: This salad dressing can be made in advance if stored in the refrigerator.*

Jo Ann Olsen
Crawford County (Grayling)

FRENCH SALAD DRESSING

1 cup sugar
1 cup catsup
1 cup white vinegar
2 cups salad oil
1 teaspoon salt
1 teaspoon Accent
3 to 4 tablespoons dehydrated onion or onion powder

Combine all ingredients and mix well. Keep in refrigerator until ready to use. Remove and let set until room temperature. Shake well before using.

Mrs. Edward Powers (Hallie)
Wexford County (Cadillac)

MUFFIN SANDWICHES

1 can Spam
1 medium onion
1 medium green pepper
1 stick Kraft Cheddar cheese
1 tablespoon butter, melted
English muffins

Grind ingredients together and spread on English muffins. Bake in 325 degree oven for 30 minutes.

Mrs. Ron Daniels (Debbe)
Gratiot County (Breckenridge)

Sandwiches

BARBECUED BEEF ON BUNS

4 or 5 pound beef roast (arm)
1 large onion, chopped
1½ cups brown sugar
2 tablespoons Worcestershire sauce
1½ tablespoons mustard
1 tablespoon chili powder
¾ cup cider vinegar
1 32-ounce bottle catsup
2 cups beef broth
24 to 30 hamburger buns

Cook roast in slow cooker or pressure cooker until tender. Pour off and reserve broth. Cool and remove grease. Cut roast into fine pieces, removing fat and gristle. In 3-quart saucepan, brown onion. Add sugar, Worcestershire sauce, mustard, chili powder and vinegar and stir until thoroughly mixed. Add catsup and beef broth. Simmer all ingredients for 30 minutes. Place cut-up beef roast in 5-quart pan. Pour barbecue sauce over meat to desired thickness. Simmer 1 hour adding more sauce if necessary. Serve on buns. *Note: Left-over roast may be used. If broth is needed, use bouillon cubes when making barbecue sauce. Sauce will keep indefinitely in glass container in refrigerator.*

Mrs. DeVere BeDour (Peggy)
Clare County (Harrison)

CRAB BURGER

1 cup crabmeat, canned or frozen and drained
1 cup mayonnaise
1 cup chili sauce
1¾ cups sharp Cheddar cheese, shredded
6 hamburger buns, split

Combine crabmeat, mayonnaise, chili sauce and 1 cup of Cheddar cheese. *Note: This can be prepared the previous day or just before needed.* Spread mixture over split hamburger buns. Sprinkle remaining shredded Cheddar cheese lightly over top and broil until just lightly brown and bubbly—about 3 minutes. Serve immediately. *Ideal for an after-the-game snack!*

Mrs. Jud Heathcote (Beverly)
Ingham County (East Lansing)

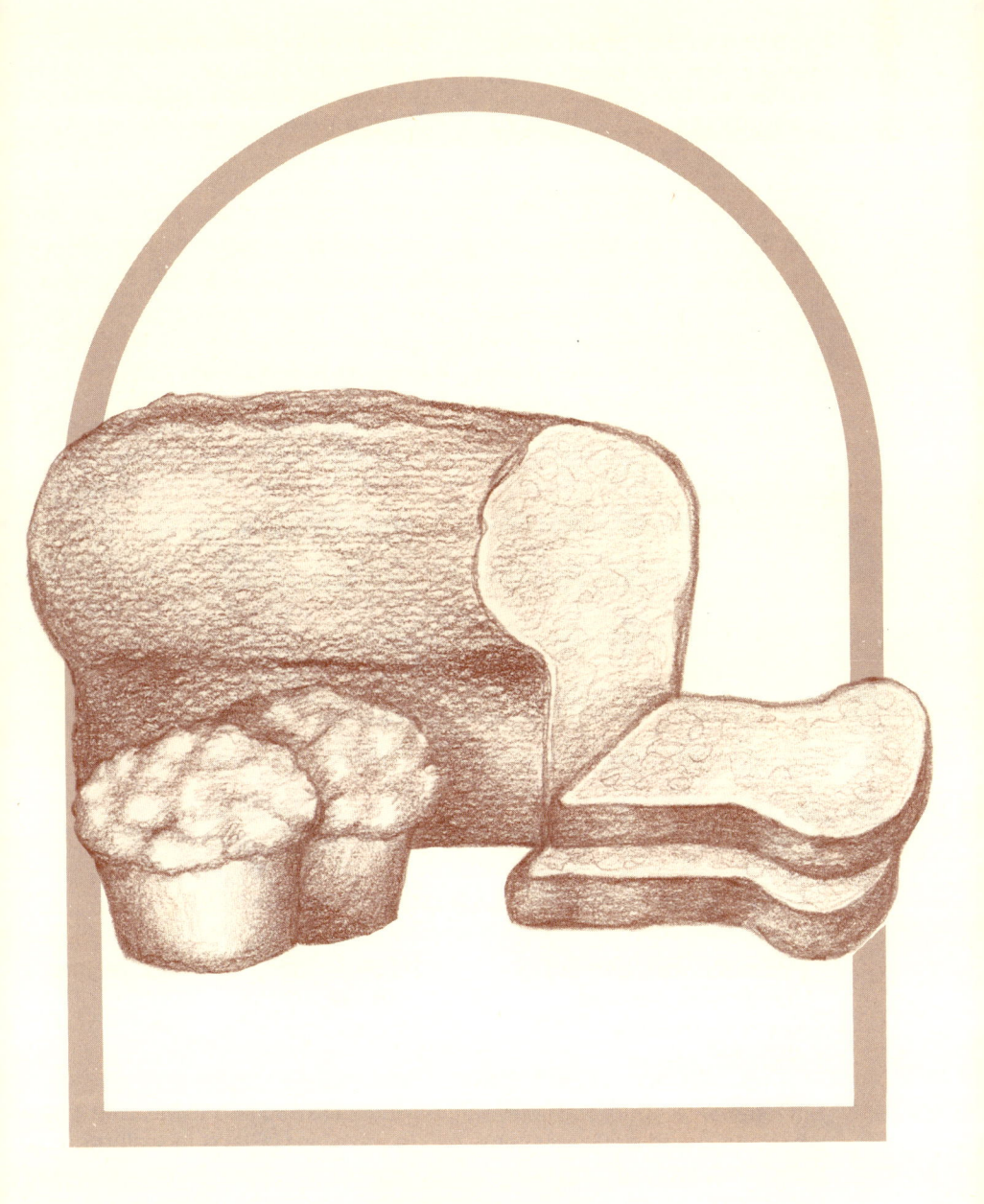

Breads

Breads

GRANDMA'S BREAD

1 cup milk, scalded
3½ cups cold water
2 large tablespoons shortening
3 tablespoons sugar

3 teaspoons salt
2 yeast cakes
5½ cups white flour
3 cups whole wheat flour

Cool scalded milk with water. Add shortening, sugar, salt and yeast. Mix well. Stir in 1 cup white flour and the 3 cups whole wheat flour; mix well. Let this mixture get light. Add remainder of white flour to knead and knead lightly. Let this mixture get light. Knead and make into 4 loaves. Put loaves into greased bread pans and let them get light. Bake at 400 degrees for 10 to 15 minutes, reduce oven to 375 degrees and bake for 40 to 45 more minutes, or until done. Let cool in pan for 5 to 10 minutes, then turn onto racks to complete cooling. Yield; 4 loaves. *Note: I usually use dry yeast in place of cakes (use 2¼-ounce packages dry yeast). This recipe was developed before the days of dry yeast. Bread is delicious when toasted and lightly buttered.*

Sara Tanis
Ingham County (Okemos)

BROWN BREAD

1 cup all-purpose flour
½ teaspoon salt
1 teaspoon baking soda
½ cup sugar
2 cups whole wheat flour, unsifted

½ cup molasses
1½ cups milk
¾ cup raisins

Sift together all-purpose flour, salt, baking soda and sugar. Mix with whole wheat flour and add molasses, milk and raisins. Place in well greased 9x5x3-inch loaf pan and bake at 375 degrees for 1 hour. *Note: This bread keeps well and is better if allowed to "ripen" overnight. Slice and spread with butter or cream cheese.*

Mrs. Walter Brown (Sue Anne)
Otsego County (Gaylord)

GRANDMA'S WHITE BREAD

3 cups whole milk
2 cakes or packages yeast
2 teaspoons sugar
4 eggs, at room temperature
4½ cups flour, sifted
¼ cup butter, melted

¼ cup Fluffo, melted
3 cups flour, sifted
2 teaspoons sugar
2 teaspoons salt
1 egg yolk
3 tablespoons milk

Heat milk to about 100 degrees. Add yeast, 2 teaspoons sugar and beaten eggs and stir until dissolved. Add 4½ cups flour and beat until smooth. Pour cooled, melted butter and Fluffo over batter. Cover with tea towel, and let stand in a warm place for 1 hour. Beat down, cover and let stand for ¾ hour. Sift 3 cups flour, 2 teaspoons sugar and salt and add to "sponge." Mix well, turn out onto floured board and knead well for 7 to 10 minutes, adding as little flour as possible. Or, if you have a mixer with a dough hook, knead for 3 to 4 minutes, until smooth, do not add additional flour. Cover bowl, stand in warm place and let rise for 1 hour. Punch down, divide into 3 parts, knead lightly and shape into loaves. Place in well greased 5x9-inch or 5x12-inch loaf pans, cover and let rise for 1 hour. For crusty, well browned, shiny tops brush with egg yolk beaten with milk. Bake at 400 degrees for 15 to 20 minutes, then reduce heat to 325 degrees and bake for 20 minutes or until done. Bottom will sound hollow when tapped. Brush tops with cold water immediately after removing from pans. Let stand on cake rack to cool. *Note: When cooled completely, loaves can be frozen if well wrapped in foil. A slight amount of defrosting and 15 minutes in a 300 degree oven will produce a "fresh" loaf of bread.*

Mrs. Patricia Andrick
Oakland County (Birmingham)

BEER BREAD

2 cups self-rising flour
2 level tablespoons sugar

1 12-ounce can beer, at room temperature

Mix all ingredients well in large mixing bowl. Batter will be sticky. Dough does not need to rise. Pour immediately into a very well-greased 1-pound size loaf pan and bake in preheated 350 degree oven for 55 to 65 minutes. *Note: Top of loaf will split and will not be too brown, but bottom and sides of loaf will be a rich, dark brown. Very good hot, break into pieces and slather with butter–smells heavenly when baking!*

Marie Kamps
Ottawa County (Hudsonville)

Joy Gallagher
Genesee County (Flint)

ALL-BRAN MUFFINS

2 cups boiling water
2 cups 100% bran (Bran Buds)
1 cup shortening
2 cups sugar
4 eggs

1 quart buttermilk
4 cups All-Bran
4 cups flour
5 teaspoons soda
1 teaspoon salt

Pour boiling water over Bran Buds and set aside. Cream shortening, sugar, and eggs. Add to buttermilk. Add All-Bran. Sift together flour, soda, and salt and add to mixture. Fold in soaked bran. Bake in 400 degree oven in greased muffin tins for 15 to 18 minutes. Yield: 4 dozen muffins. *Note: Batter will keep in refrigerator at least 2 weeks. Bake as needed.*

Mrs. Clifford Lumbert (Nola)
Clinton County (St. Johns)

CRESCENT REFRIGERATOR ROLLS

1 package dry yeast
¼ cup lukewarm water
6 tablespoons sugar
½ teaspoon salt

6 tablespoons butter or margarine
1 cup boiling water
1 egg
4 cups all-purpose flour

Pour dry yeast into ¼ cup lukewarm water and set aside. In large mixing bowl, pour 1 cup boiling water over the sugar, salt and butter. Let stand about 5 minutes to cool to warm. Beat in the whole egg and the yeast mixture. Stir with large spoon and add 2 cups flour, mixing until smooth. Gradually add remaining 2 cups of flour, stirring constantly. Let dough rise in covered bowl for approximately 2 hours in warm spot. (Oven which was heated for 1 minute and heat turned off is very good). Push dough down and refrigerate for at least 4 hours. When ready to use, push dough down and cut in either 2 or 4 parts. Roll each part into a 9 to 10-inch circle. Butter and cut into 8 wedge-shaped pieces. Roll wedge from wide end to a point, tucking the point under as it is placed on cookie sheet. Turn ends in to give a crescent shape. Place on buttered cookie sheet. Let rise for 1½ hours. Bake at 400 degrees for 20 minutes. Yield: 16 large or 32 small rolls.

Mrs. H. Dan Vander Molen (Agnes)
Ottawa County (Jenison)

GRAMMA'S BREAKFAST POPOVERS

Butter or margarine for muffin pan
6 eggs
1 cup milk
2 cups flour
2 teaspoons salt

Preheat oven to 400 degrees. Place ½ teaspoon butter or margarine in each muffin cup and place in oven to heat while mixing ingredients. Beat eggs together, and add milk. Mix well. Add flour and salt; mix well. Fill hot muffin cups ½ full with batter and place on middle rack in oven. Bake at 400 degrees for 30 to 35 minutes, or until well-browned. Serve hot with plenty of butter and jam. Yield: 12 popovers. *Note: Popovers will rise high above muffin cups and should be well-browned to ensure crispness. Recipe can be divided evenly for single batch.*

Mrs. Carl Schultz (Joyce)
Kalkaska County (Kalkaska)

YELLOW ROLLS

⅓ cup dry corn meal (yellow)
1 teaspoon salt
½ cup sugar
½ cup margarine
2 cups milk
2 eggs, beaten
1 package dried yeast softened in ¼ cup warm water with 2 teaspoons sugar added
4 to 5 cups flour to make a soft dough

Combine corn meal, salt, sugar, margarine and milk in top of double boiler. Cook until medium thick. Put aside and let cool until lukewarm. Add eggs and yeast mixture. Then add flour to make a soft dough. Turn out on a well-floured board and knead well. Put in a greased bowl, cover and let rise until double in bulk. Divide dough to handle easier and roll out to ½-inch thickness. Cut into rounds with biscuit cutter. Brush ½ of each round with melted margarine, dent center with knife and fold over. Place on greased pans. Brush tops with melted margarine, cover and let rise until double in bulk. Bake at 375 degrees for 12 to 15 minutes. *Note: These can be baked until they begin to brown around the edges, taken from the oven and frozen. Remove any number you desire, place in oven and brown for fresh rolls.*

Mrs. Raymond Benson (Elizabeth)
Cheboygan County (Topinabee)

Breads

REFRIGERATOR ROLLS

2 cups warm water
2 packages Red Star yeast
¼ cup sugar
2 teaspoons salt

6½ to 7 cups flour, sifted and divided
1 egg
¼ cup margarine, softened

Dissolve yeast in warm water. Add sugar, salt and about half the flour. Beat well by hand or with mixer at high speed. Add egg and soft margarine and beat well again. Add remaining flour with a spoon to make a soft dough. Place in a greased bowl and turn to grease the top. Cover with a damp towel and a lid and store in the refrigerator overnight or up to 5 days. Remove from refrigerator 2½ hours before baking time and shape as desired. Place in well-greased baking pan and let rise in a warm place (at least 72 degrees). If kitchen is cool, set over a pan of hot water and cover both with a large towel. Bake rolls 12 to 15 minutes at 400 degrees or until golden brown. Brush tops with melted butter or margarine.

Mrs. Lester C. Fales
Antrim County (Kewadin)

GOTHKA ROLLS

1 cake compressed yeast, or 1 package dry yeast
¼ cup warm water
¾ cup sugar
1 cup butter or margarine, melted

4 eggs at room temperature
1 cup condensed milk
5 cups flour, unsifted
Sesame, Caraway or poppy seeds

Add yeast to warm water to soften. Cream sugar and butter. Blend in the eggs. Add the milk and the softened yeast blend. Add the flour to make a soft kneadable dough. Grease the bowl and the top of the dough. Let rise until double in bulk. Take small piece of dough and roll out like a pencil. Shape into a braid on cookie sheet. Wet the top of the braid with condensed milk and sprinkle with your favorite seeds such as Sesame, Caraway or poppy seeds. Let rise until double in bulk. Bake at 350 degrees for 10 to 12 minutes. May be frozen for later use.

Mary Jane Dorner
Lapeer County (Columbiaville)

HAMBURGER BUNS

½ cup margarine, melted
1 2-ounce yeast cake
¼ cup lukewarm water
2 tablespoons sugar
1 cup milk, scalded or 1 cup hot water and 1 cup dry powdered milk
⅓ cup sugar
1 teaspoon salt
2 eggs, slightly beaten
5 to 5½ cups flour

Melt margarine and set aside. Split the yeast in half and dissolve in lukewarm water with 2 tablespoons sugar in it. Set aside to rise. Combine in a large bowl the scalded milk (or 1 cup hot water and 1 cup dry powdered milk), sugar and salt. Blend in slightly beaten eggs and melted margarine. Add yeast and gradually add flour to form stiff dough. Knead on a floured board or cloth for a few minutes. Dough can be a bit sticky. If you don't need this amount of flour, don't use it, if you need more, use it. Then place dough in a greased bowl, cover and let rise in a warm place (85 to 90 degrees) until double in bulk, about 1½ to 2 hours. Punch down and let rise 1 hour longer. Remove from bowl and place on a lightly floured board. Shape into oblong pieces and slice into 24 to 28 pieces. Shape into buns, then flatten out with rolling pin. Place on greased cookie sheet and grease top of buns. Cover with waxed paper and clean towel and let rise until double in bulk, 1 hour or more. Bake at 400 degrees for 20 minutes until golden brown. Yield: 24 or more buns depending on size desired. *Note: These buns are delicious split and toasted in a toaster. They can also be used for dinner buns. Shape in round buns and place in greased round or square pan.*

Mrs. Kenneth Dickinson (Helen)
St. Clair County (Port Huron)

. . . Bread has risen enough when 2 fingertips pressed on top leave an indentation.

Breads

APPLESAUCE NUT BREAD

2 tablespoons shortening
¾ cup sugar
1 egg
1 cup applesauce
2 cups flour

1 teaspoon salt
½ teaspoon soda
3 teaspoons baking powder
½ teaspoon cinnamon
1 cup walnuts, chopped

Combine ingredients in order given. Mix well and bake in loaf pan at 350 degrees for 50 minutes.

Mrs. Allan Baldwin (Avis)
St. Joseph County (Three Rivers)

. . . Sprinkle 1 teaspoon of sugar on yeast dissolved in water to check for yeast freshness. Fresh yeast will produce a foam.

BANANA LOAF

⅔ cup white sugar
⅓ cup shortening, softened
2 eggs
3 tablespoons sour milk
1 cup bananas, mashed

2 cups flour
1 teaspoon baking powder
½ teaspoon baking soda
½ teaspoon salt
½ cup nuts, chopped (Optional)

Mix together thoroughly, sugar and shortening. Add eggs, beating in thoroughly. Stir in sour milk and mix in mashed bananas. Sift together flour, baking powder, baking soda and salt. Add flour mixture to creamed mixture and mix very thoroughly. Add nuts. Pour into well-greased loaf pan. Let stand for 20 minutes before baking. Bake at 350 degrees for 55 minutes, until well browned and wooden pick inserted in center of loaf comes out clean. Take loaf out of pan when done baking and cover with towel.

Valeria J. Blake
Kalkaska County (Kalkaska)

BANANA BREAD

1 stick margarine, melted
1½ cups sugar
2 eggs
¾ cup sour milk
1 cup bananas, mashed (3 bananas)

2 cups flour
1 teaspoon salt
1 teaspoon soda
½ teaspoon baking powder
½ cup nuts, chopped

Cream melted margarine and sugar. Add eggs one at a time, beating thoroughly after each addition. Add sour milk and beat. Add mashed bananas and beat. Stir in flour, salt, soda and baking powder. Add nut meats and stir. Pour batter into 2 greased and floured 9⅝x5½x2¾ loaf pans. Bake in 350 degree oven for 35 to 40 minutes.

Jean R. MacNicol
Montmorency County (Hillman)

PINEAPPLE POPPINS

Batter:
2 cups all-purpose flour, sifted
3 teaspoons baking powder
½ teaspoon salt
½ cup sugar
¼ cup margarine or butter, melted

1 egg, beaten
¾ cup milk
¼ cup pineapple juice
1¼ cups pineapple tidbits

Drain pineapple, reserving ¼ cup juice. Set aside. Sift flour, baking powder, salt and sugar together in large mixing bowl. Thoroughly combine melted margarine or butter, egg, milk and pineapple juice in small bowl. Add to dry ingredients and mix until just blended. Fill 12 paper or well-greased muffin cups. Place 5 tidbits around edge and center of filled cups. *Note: Pineapple slices cut into tidbit sizes may be substituted, but crushed pineapple is not recommended.*

Topping:
½ cup all-purpose flour, sifted
¼ teaspoon cinnamon

⅓ cup brown sugar
¼ cup margarine or butter, melted

Mix flour, cinnamon, and sugar. Add melted margarine or butter and blend. Sprinkle this mixture over muffins. Bake in 375 degree oven for 30 minutes. Serve hot with butter.

Mrs. Wilbur Troth (Jewel)
Branch County (Bronson)

CARROT-PINEAPPLE BREAD

3 eggs, beaten
2 cups sugar
1 cup cooking oil
1 cup carrots, grated
1 cup crushed pineapple, undrained
1 cup nuts, chopped
2 teaspoons vanilla
1½ teaspoons cinnamon
1 teaspoon soda
1 teaspoon salt
3 cups flour

Mix in order eggs, sugar, oil, carrots, pineapple, nuts and vanilla. Sift together cinnamon, soda, salt and flour and add to mixture. Pour into two 9x5-inch loaf pans lined with waxed paper. Bake at 325 degrees for 1 hour.

Mrs. Stan Van Antwerp
Ottawa County (Hudsonville)

PUMPKIN NUT BREAD

3½ cups flour, sifted
2 teaspoons baking soda
1½ teaspoons salt
1 teaspoon cinnamon
1 teaspoon nutmeg
3 cups white sugar
¾ cup nutmeats, chopped
4 eggs, slightly beaten
1½ cups pumpkin
1 cup oil
⅔ cup water

Combine flour, soda, salt, cinnamon, nutmeg and sugar and mix well. Add nuts and mix. Combine slightly beaten eggs, pumpkin, oil and water in a separate bowl and mix well. Pour egg mixture into flour mixture all at once and blend until smooth. Spoon batter into 2 greased 10¼x3⅝x2⅝ pans. Bake in preheated 350 degree oven for 1 hour. *Note: Candied fruit can be added at holiday time to the batter before the batter is poured into the pans. Breads can be decorated with candied fruits and nuts to make lovely presents.*

Ann Marie Arcieri
St. Clair County (Port Huron)

RAISIN NUT BREAD

2 cups seedless raisins
2½ cups boiling water
1 tablespoon margarine or lard
2½ teaspoons soda
1 teaspoon vanilla

1½ cups sugar
1 teaspoon salt
3 eggs
4 cups flour
1 cup nuts, chopped

Combine raisins, boiling water, and margarine and let stand 2 to 3 hours or overnight. Stir in soda, vanilla, sugar, salt and flour. Add eggs one at a time beating thoroughly after each addition. Add nuts. Bake in 2 loaf pans at 375 degrees for 10 minutes. Reduce heat to 350 degrees and continue baking for 50 minutes.

Ann Bartholomew
Kalkaska County (Kalkaska)

. . . Heat raisins in a dish over low heat or hot water before adding to bread batter. This keeps them from sinking to bottom of batter.

RHUBARB BREAD

1½ cups brown sugar
⅔ cup oil
1 egg
1½ cups rhubarb, diced
2½ cups flour

1 teaspoon salt
1 teaspoon baking soda
1 cup buttermilk
1 teaspoon vanilla

Mix brown sugar and oil. Add egg and mix well. Add the diced rhubarb. Sift together the flour, salt and baking soda. Add the flour mixture alternately with the buttermilk and vanilla. Bake at 350 degrees for 1 hour. *Note: ½ cup nutmeats may be added if desired.*

Mrs. James Elliott (Marlene)
Berrien County (Stevensville)

Breads

ZUCCHINI BREAD

3 eggs, slightly beaten
2 cups sugar
1 cup oil
3 cups flour
1 teaspoon salt
1 teaspoon baking powder

3 teaspoons cinnamon
2 cups unpeeled zucchini, grated or chopped
1 cup nuts, coarsely chopped
3 teaspoons vanilla

Combine eggs, sugar and oil. Sift flour, salt, baking powder and cinnamon and add to egg mixture. Stir to blend well and add zucchini, nuts and vanilla. Divide batter into 2 greased loaf pans and bake at 350 degrees for about 1 hour, until top springs back.

Mrs. Richard S. Allen, Sr.
Clare County (Clare)

Mrs. Lawrence E. Erwin (Lillian)
Ogemaw County (Lupton)

Mary Jane Nobel
Tuscola County (Fairgrove)

Geraldine Horton
Kalkaska County (Kalkaska)

... If you need extra counter space when baking, pull out a drawer and cover with your pastry board.

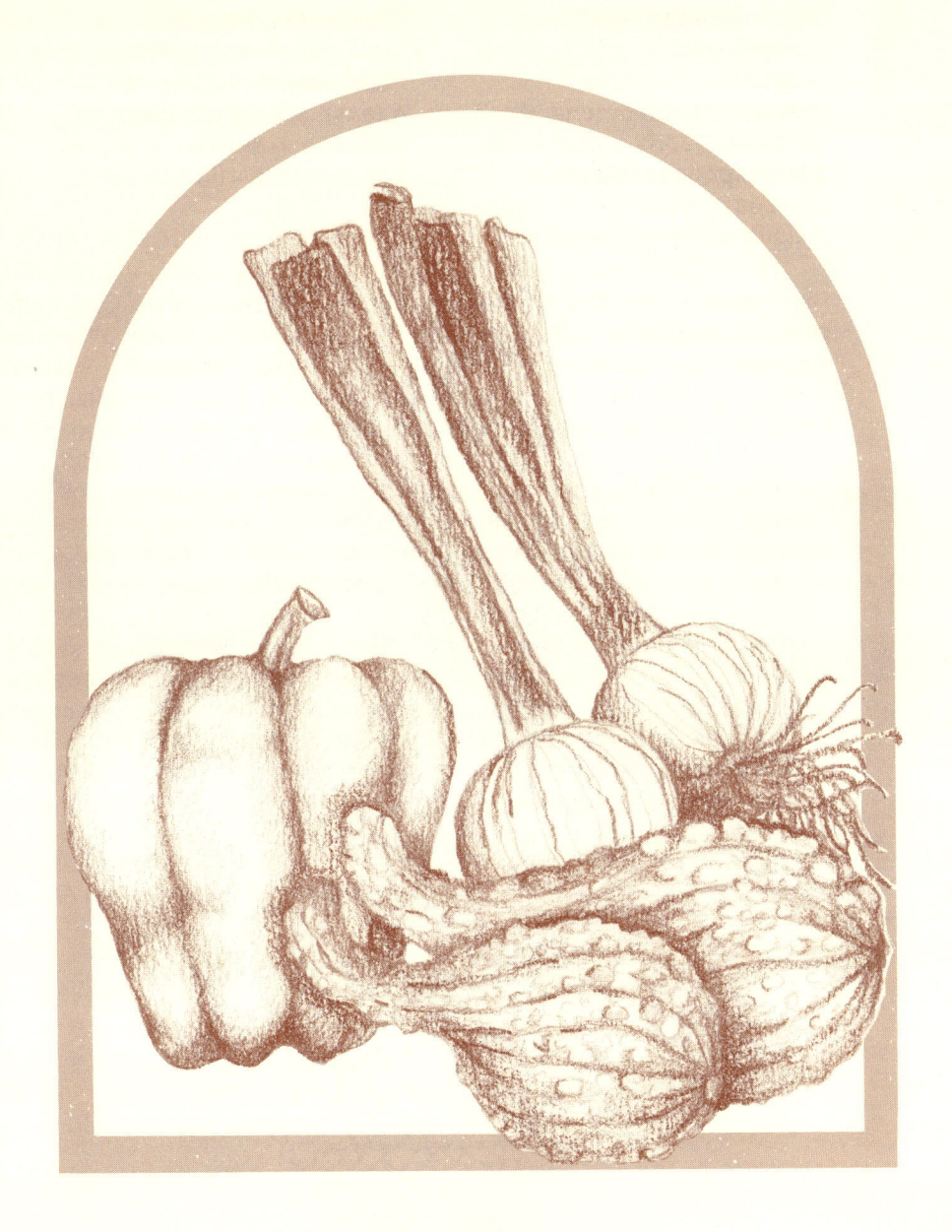

Vegetables

Vegetables

AU SABLE BAKED BEANS

2 pounds dried pea beans
1 pound thick-sliced smoked bacon
3 large Spanish onions, diced
3½ tablespoons brown sugar
3 tablespoons molasses
3 tablespoons Hickory smoke flavored barbecue sauce

2 teaspoons Worcestershire sauce
2 teaspoons liquid smoke
1 teaspoon seasoned salt
½ teaspoon dry mustard
½ teaspoon seasoned pepper
½ teaspoon garlic powder

Rinse pea beans well and place into pot or 6-quart Dutch oven. Cover with generous excess of water. Soak overnight. In the morning, pour off excess water until the beans are covered with about ½ inch of water. Cut bacon strips into 1-inch widths and sauté over low heat until just beginning to brown. Transfer bacon into the bean pot, retaining the bacon grease in the frying pan. Sauté the diced onions in the bacon grease. Add Worcestershire sauce to the onions when they are nearly browned and transfer onion mixture into the bean pot. Add the brown sugar, molasses, barbecue sauce, smoke sauce, seasoned salt, dry mustard, seasoned pepper and garlic powder to the bean pot and stir to mix thoroughly. Place covered pot in 300 degree oven and bake for 4 to 6 hours. Yield: about 4 quarts of baked beans, enough for 8 hungry fishermen or 35 dieting ladies. *Note: Beans should always be slightly covered with liquid. Add water if needed to keep the baking beans slightly covered. Since taste preferences of various cooks differ, the seasoning, particularly the amount of salt, should be adjusted to taste. Sampling the liquid often during cooking and adjusting to your personal preference is suggested.*

Nathaniel H. Rowe, D.D.S.
Washtenaw County (Ann Arbor)

BROCCOLI-CHEESE-RICE CASSEROLE

1 stick margarine
½ cup onion, chopped
½ cup green pepper, chopped
½ cup celery, chopped
1 16½-ounce can cream of mushroom soup
1 small jar Cheez Whiz
1½ pounds fresh broccoli (or 2 packages frozen cut-up broccoli)
2 cups rice, cooked
Potato chips, crushed

Sauté onion, green pepper and celery in margarine in frying pan. Cook until tender. Add cream of mushroom soup, Cheez Whiz and broccoli and stir. Add rice and mix well. Place mixture in 2-quart casserole dish and top with crushed potato chips. Bake at 350 degrees for 45 minutes to 1 hour.

Wealtha Witer
Gladwin County (Gladwin)

CABBAGE ROLLS

1 head cabbage, cored
1 pound lean ground beef
1 medium onion, grated
1 clove garlic, crushed
1 medium egg, beaten
¼ cup tomato juice
¼ cup Matzo meal or fine cracker crumbs
2 cups water or tomato juice

Steam cabbage in boiling water until leaves separate and are soft enough to roll. Devein by skinning large vein off leaf on top, but do not cut through leaf. Mix ground beef, onion, garlic, egg, tomato juice and meal or crackers well. Roll ⅓ cup of meat mixture in a cabbage leaf with sides folded in. Cabbage roll should look like an egg roll. Shred unused cabbage with a diced onion and spread in bottom of 9x13-inch Pyrex dish to make a bedding. Place cabbage rolls in saucepan seam side down with 2 cups of water or tomato juice. Cook at medium heat for about 1 hour on top of stove. Remove cabbage rolls to 9x13-inch Pyrex pan on top of cabbage and onion bedding. Cover with sauce below and bake at 350 degrees for 2 hours. Turn cabbage rolls carefully about every 20 minutes to brown evenly.

Sauce:
8 ounces tomato sauce
½ cup brown sugar
1 teaspoon citric acid
⅛ teaspoon pepper
½ teaspoon salt

Combine ingredients and pour over cabbage rolls. *Note: Additional citric acid and brown sugar can be added to sauce to suit your taste.*

Mrs. Ben Brot
Kalamazoo County (Kalamazoo)

Vegetables

CARROT CASSEROLE

1 cup water chestnuts, cut and drained
4 cups carrots, cooked, sliced and drained
1 cup mushroom soup
1 medium jar Cheez Whiz
1 package sliced almonds
1 can onion rings, crushed

Cut and drain water chestnuts. Cook and drain carrots. Mix all ingredients together except onion rings and place in Pyrex dish. Cover with crushed onion rings. Bake at 350 degrees for 30 minutes.

Daleta Pontack
Clinton County (Elsie)

CASSEROLE OF CELERY

3 cups celery, sliced
Buttered bread crumbs
½ cup slivered almonds
1 can cream of chicken soup, undiluted
1 small can water chestnuts, sliced

Cook celery in salted water until fork-tender. Butter the bread crumbs and add almonds. Drain celery and add undiluted soup and water chestnuts. Pour into buttered 1-quart casserole and top with bread crumbs and almond mixture. Place in preheated 350 degree oven and bake until dish is bubbly and crumbs are golden brown.

Mrs. Warren S. Bennett (Bertee)
Iosco County (Tawas City)

EXOTIC CELERY

4 heaping cups celery, cut in 1-inch pieces
1 can cream of chicken soup
1 can pimento, undrained and chopped
1 can water chestnuts, sliced and drained
1 cup sliced almonds

Cut celery in 1-inch pieces diagonally and cook in salted water for 8 minutes. Drain. Add cream of chicken soup, pimento and water chestnuts. Mix all ingredients together well and place in greased 8x8-inch casserole. Top with sautéed sliced almonds. Bake at 350 degrees for 30 to 45 minutes uncovered. Serves 4.

Catherine L. Houston
Ingham County (Lansing)

CUCUMBERS AU GRATIN

3 medium cucumbers, peeled and diced
2 tablespoons butter
2 tablespoons flour
1¼ cups milk
1 bouillon cube
¼ teaspoon onion juice or grated onion
Salt and pepper
1 cup mild cheese, grated
½ cup buttered bread crumbs

Cook cucumbers about 5 minutes in barely enough salted boiling water to cover. Drain well. Make a cream sauce of butter, flour and milk, stirring constantly until smooth. Stir in bouillon cube and onion. Season sauce to taste after bouillon cube is completely dissolved. Add cheese and simmer until melted, stirring constantly. Add cucumbers and pour in small greased casserole. Top with buttered bread crumbs and bake at 350 degrees about 20 minutes or until browned. Serves 6.

Mrs. Ben Lowell (Patricia)
Ottawa County (Grand Haven)

. . . Cover peeled potatoes with water, add a few drops of vinegar and refrigerate. Potatoes will keep from 3 to 4 days.

GREEN BEAN CASSEROLE

2 12-ounce packages frozen French style green beans
3 tablespoons butter, melted
2 tablespoons flour
1 teaspoon salt
¼ teaspoon pepper
1 teaspoon sugar
½ teaspoon onion, grated
1 cup dairy sour cream
½ pound Cheddar cheese, grated
½ cup Corn Flake crumbs

Cook green beans according to directions; drain. Combine butter and flour and cook gently. Remove from heat and stir in salt, pepper, sugar, onion and sour cream. Fold in green beans and place in a shallow 2-quart casserole. Cover with grated cheese and top with Corn Flake crumbs that have been mixed with 1 tablespoon melted butter. Bake at 350 degrees for 30 minutes. Serves 8. *Note: A good vegetable dish for buffets too.*

Arletta Hamilton
Newaygo County (Fremont)

Vegetables

GREEN BEANS

2 cans French green beans, drained
1 can tomatoes, drained
4 tablespoons salad dressing
2 tablespoons Worcestershire sauce
3 drops Tabasco
1 onion, diced
6 slices bacon, browned and crumbled

Combine all ingredients together and mix well. Bake at 350 degrees for 45 minutes.

Nan Poquette
Ingham County (East Lansing)

ONION PIE

30 saltine crackers, crushed
½ cup butter
3 cups onions, thinly sliced
¼ cup butter
½ pound Cheddar cheese
1½ cups milk, scalded
3 eggs, beaten
½ teaspoon salt
½ teaspoon pepper

Make crust of saltines and ½ cup butter, placing in 10x10-inch pan. Sauté onions in the ¼ cup butter. Place on crust and sprinle with grated Cheddar cheese. When ready to bake, scald milk with beaten eggs, salt and pepper. Bake at 350 degrees for 30 to 45 minutes.

Mrs. Jacob Ponstein
Ottawa County (Grand Haven)

POTATO GOODIE

2 pounds frozen hash brown potatoes (nuggets)
1 can cream of mushroom soup, undiluted
½ cup onion, diced
1 16-ounce carton sour cream
1 stick margarine, melted
8 ounces sharp Cheddar cheese, grated
Salt and pepper to taste

Thaw potatoes for 30 minutes. Mix all ingredients together in a large mixing bowl. Place mixture in 9x13-inch baking dish and bake at 375 degrees for 1 hour. Serves 12 to 16.

Robert A. Fisher
Ingham County (East Lansing)

BERTA POTATOES

8 medium size potatoes, cooked, cooled and grated
½ stick margarine
2 cups medium sharp cheese, grated
2 cups sour cream
⅓ cup green onions, chopped
¼ teaspoon pepper
1 teaspoon salt
½ teaspoon butter, melted to pour over top

Cook potatoes and cool well before grating. Add all ingredients and mix well.

Robert A. Peterson
Jackson County (Jackson)

SUMMER SQUASH CASSEROLE

6 cups yellow crooked neck summer squash, chopped
1 small onion, chopped
½ teaspoon salt
1 cup dairy sour cream
1 10¾-ounce can cream of chicken soup
1 cup carrots, shredded
1 cup butter or margarine, melted
1 6 or 8-ounce box herb seasoned stuffing mix, chicken flavored

Combine chopped, deseeded squash, chopped onion and salt in a small amount of water and cook for 5 minutes or until tender. Drain. Combine sour cream, cream of chicken soup and shredded carrots; fold in drained squash and onion. Combine melted butter or margarine with herb seasoned stuffing. Spread ½ of this mixture in greased 12x7½x2-inch baking dish. Spoon vegetable mixture on top. Cover with remaining ½ of stuffing mixture. Bake at 350 degrees for 30 minutes. Serves 8 to 10.

Mrs. Roland Church (Ardath)
Ogemaw County (Rose City)

Vegetables

STEWED TOMATO CASSEROLE

3 slices toast, buttered and sprinkled with garlic powder
3 tablespoons butter or margarine
1 medium onion, chopped
3 stalks celery, chopped
½ green pepper, chopped
1 35-ounce can tomatoes
2 teaspoons sugar
1 teaspoon oregano
½ teaspoon Bouquet Garni
Salt and pepper to taste

Generously butter a 2-quart casserole. Drop in toast broken in small pieces. Sauté in butter the onion, celery, and green pepper in small pan until soft. Add tomatoes, sugar, oregano, Bouquet Garni, salt and pepper to onion mixture and mix together. Place in casserole over toast. Bake at 350 degrees until bubbly and thick, about 1 hour. Serves 6 to 8. *Note: Grated Parmesan cheese may be added to top before baking.*

Mrs. Joseph Wisniewski (Rosemary)
Genesee County (Flint)

. . . A hole poked through the center of an onion will prevent onion center from popping out while cooking.

VEGETABLE MEDLEY

2 cups carrots, sliced
2 cups zucchini, sliced
1½ cups onion, sliced
¾ cup green pepper, sliced
2 cups celery, sliced
2 tablespoons sugar
3 tablespoons cornstarch
2 teaspoons salt
¼ teaspoon pepper
2 cups canned tomatoes
4 tablespoons butter or margarine

Grease a 3-quart casserole. Place ½ of the sliced carrots, zucchini, onions, green pepper and celery in the casserole; sprinkle with ½ of the sugar, cornstarch, salt and pepper. Repeat this process with the remaining ½ of the sliced vegetables, sugar, cornstarch, salt and pepper. Pour 2 cups of canned tomatoes over all and dot with 4 tablespoons of butter. Cover and bake at 350 degrees for 1½ hours. Serves 10.

Mrs. R. J. Lichtenfelt (Barbara)
Isabella County (Weidman)

VEGETABLE MEDLEY CASSEROLE

- 1 10¾-ounce can cream of celery soup, undiluted
- 1 8-ounce jar Cheez-Whiz
- 1 3-ounce package cream cheese
- 1 stick margarine
- 2 20-ounce packages frozen California vegetables
- 1 10-ounce package frozen kernel corn
- 1 8-ounce package herbed stuffing mix

Warm celery soup, Cheez-Whiz, cream cheese and 2 ounces margarine in top of double boiler until well blended. Combine unthawed vegetables in large mixing bowl. Pour sauce over vegetables and toss well to coat all pieces. Pour mixture into large baking pan or casserole dish. Bake at 350 degrees for 40 minutes. Melt remaining margarine and toss stuffing mix in margarine. Spread stuffing mixture over vegetable mixture and bake an additional 20 minutes at 350 degrees. Serves 12.

Robert A. Fisher
Ingham County (East Lansing)

. . . Place a heel of bread over cabbage before placing lid on pot and cooking to eliminate odors. Good for cooking Brussels sprouts and broccoli also.

VEGETABLE CASSEROLE

- 1½ cups cauliflower, in pieces
- 1½ cups broccoli, in pieces
- 1½ cups Brussels sprouts
- 2 10¾-ounce cans cream of mushroom soup
- ½ cup milk
- 1½ cups cut green beans
- 1½ cups asparagus, in pieces
- 1 small can mushrooms, drained
- Salt and pepper to taste
- ½ cup Cheddar cheese, shredded

Cook vegetables in boiling water until just tender and crisp. Drain well. Turn into greased casserole and salt and pepper to taste. Add soup, milk, and mushrooms. Stir gently. Top with cheese. Cover and bake at 325 degrees for 20 minutes or until bubbly.

Mrs. Robert Lutze
Montmorency County (Hillman)

Vegetables

YUMMY YAMS

6 medium yams
⅓ cup butter, melted
4 large apples, cored and thinly sliced
¾ cup light brown sugar, packed
½ cup slivered almonds
½ cup mandarin orange sections
½ cup orange-flavored liqueur

Preheat oven to 400 degrees. Boil yams with jackets on about 15 minutes, or until almost tender. Drain and cool. Butter an 11x7x1½-inch baking dish. Peel and slice yams. Place a layer of yams in the dish, then a layer of apples and sprinkle with brown sugar. Continue layering until yams and apples are used up. Sprinkle with almonds. Arrange mandarin oranges on top. Drizzle butter over top and pour the liqueur over top. Bake for 35 minutes. Serves 6.

Mrs. Gerald W. Zinger (Anita)
Wayne County (Dearborn)

ZUCCHINI AND CHEESE CASSEROLE

4 cups zucchini squash, sliced
½ cup onion, chopped
¼ cup salad oil
1 egg
1 cup evaporated milk
½ teaspoon salt
⅛ teaspoon pepper
1 slice white bread, broken
1 cup sharp Cheddar cheese, grated

Cook squash and onion in oil until tender. Beat egg. Add the evaporated milk, salt, pepper and bread. Alternate layers of squash, Cheddar cheese and milk mixture in a 2-quart casserole. Bake at 350 degrees for 45 minutes. Yield: 6 servings.

Beverly Stokke
Marquette County (Marquette)

Fish and Poultry

Fish

OYSTERS ROCKEFELLER

3 pounds chopped spinach
½ pound butter
1 bunch shallots
1 teaspoon thyme
1½ cups bread crumbs

3 ounces Herbseint or Pernod
4 dozen oysters, drained
¾ cup parsley
Salt, pepper and cayenne to taste

Cook spinach per package directions and drain well. Put aside. Melt butter and sauté shallots and thyme. Add bread crumbs and sauté and stir until crumbs are toasted. Then add Herbseint or Pernod, mixing thoroughly. Add drained oysters and simmer until oysters curl at edges. Then add parsley and spinach and season to taste. Place in shallow casserole dish and bake for 20 to 25 minutes.

Rusty Staub
Detroit Tigers
Owner, Rusty's, New York City

. . . To remove "Fishy" odor from house, place a piece of orange peel on the side of a stove burner and turn it on low.

SHRIMP AND CHEESE CASSEROLE

6 slices bread
½ pound Old English cheese
1 pound prepared shrimp
   (ready to eat)
¼ cup margarine, melted

3 whole eggs, beaten
½ teaspoon dry mustard
Salt to taste
1 pint milk

Break bread in pieces about the size of a quarter. Break cheese in bite-size pieces. Arrange shrimp, bread and cheese in several layers in greased casserole. Pour melted margarine over this mixture. Beat eggs. Add mustard and salt to the eggs. Then add the milk. Mix together and pour this over ingredients in casserole. Let stand a minimum of 3 hours, but preferably overnight in refrigerator, covered. Bake at 350 degrees for 1 hour, covered. *Note: More shrimp may be used if desired.*

Mrs. William G. Milliken
Wife of Governor, State of Michigan
Ingham County (Lansing)

SCALLOPED OYSTERS

Fish

1 quart oysters, drained
¾ cup oyster liquid
½ cup butter
2 tablespoons flour
1 teaspoon salt
⅛ teaspoon pepper
1¼ cups fine cracker crumbs
2 tablespoons green pepper, minced
2 tablespoons onion, minced
½ clove garlic, pressed
1 tablespoon lemon juice
1 teaspoon Worcestershire sauce

Warm oysters in liquid over low heat. Meanwhile, melt butter. Blend in flour. Add remaining ingredients except for ¼ cup of cracker crumbs. Combine mixture with oysters and liquid. Turn into greased, shallow baking dish. Sprinkle with remaining ¼ cup cracker crumbs. Bake at 375 degrees for about 20 minutes, or until light golden brown and bubbly. Yield: 6 to 8 servings.

Mrs. Gerard T. O'Brien (Pat)
Kent County (Grand Rapids)

. . . Drop fresh celery leaves into pot of boiling shrimp to destroy shrimp odor.

BAKED SHRIMP AND SCALLOPS

½ pound butter
2 tablespoons green onions, minced
4 tablespoons flour
½ cup chicken broth
2 tablespoons celery, minced
1 tablespoon parsley, minced
¼ cup dry sherry
1 teaspoon rosemary
½ teaspoon marjoram
Salt
Pepper
1 pound shrimp, shelled and deveined
1 pound scallops
1 cup water chestnuts, sliced
½ pound mushrooms, sliced
1 cup bread crumbs

Melt butter in saucepan and sauté green onions. Blend in flour and add broth, celery, parsley, sherry and seasonings. Bring to a boil, stirring slowly. Add seafood, water chestnuts, mushrooms and bread crumbs. Remove from heat and place on a well-buttered sheet of aluminum foil and seal. Place on a baking ⸱et and bake at 350 degrees for 30 minutes. Serve on a bed of seasoɩ ⸱ce. Serves 6 to 8.

Mrs. Brian Watson (Muriel)
St. Clair County (Port Huron)

SHELLFISH SORRENTO

1 8-ounce package macaroni
2 10-ounce cans mushroom soup
1 cup milk
1 5-ounce can shrimp
¼ cup pimento, minced
1 teaspoon garlic salt
⅛ teaspoon cayenne pepper
1 cup sharp cheese, grated
1 3-ounce can mushrooms
2 tablespoons butter

Cook macaroni. Heat soup with milk until bubbly. Add macaroni, shrimp, pimento, mushrooms, garlic salt, cayenne pepper and ½ cup of the cheese. Spoon into a 13x9x2-inch baking dish. Sprinkle with the rest of the cheese and dot with butter. Bake at 350 degrees until bubbly and cheese is melted and golden brown. Serves 10 to 12.

Mrs. Hugh Smith (Fern)
Iosco County (East Tawas)

. . . Use a small crochet hook to devein shrimp.

CRAB SUPREME

1 cup celery, chopped
8 slices bread, divided
1 can crabmeat
1 yellow onion, chopped
½ cup mayonnaise
½ cup green pepper
4 eggs, beaten
3 cups milk
1 cup canned mushroom soup
½ cup cheese, grated
½ teaspoon paprika

Cook celery slowly 10 minutes in a little water. Drain and reserve. Dice ½ of the bread in a baking dish. Mix crab, onion, mayonnaise, green pepper and celery and spread over bread. Dice the rest of the bread and place over crab mixture. Mix eggs and milk together and pour over dish. Cover and place in refrigerator overnight. Bake at 325 degrees for 15 minutes. Spoon soup over the top. Sprinkle with cheese and paprika. Bake for 1 hour more or until golden brown. Serves 8. *Note: This should be made a day ahead of time.*

Janet Wood
Cross Plains, Wisconsin

CRABMEAT AND MUSHROOM CASSEROLE

2 6½-ounce cans crabmeat
1 4½-ounce can whole mushrooms
3 tablespoons butter
2 tablespoons flour
½ teaspoon dry mustard
¼ teaspoon dry tarragon
½ cup sour cream
½ cup dry Vermouth
¼ cup Cheddar cheese, grated
½ cup bread crumbs

Drain crabmeat and mushrooms. Make cream sauce by melting butter, blending in flour, mustard and tarragon, and adding cream and Vermouth slowly. Heat sauce over low heat until smooth and thick but do not boil. Stir sauce as it thickens. Add crabmeat and mushrooms to sauce. Place in casserole. Mix bread crumbs and grated cheese and sprinkle over the top of the food in the casserole. Bake, uncovered for 30 to 40 minutes at 350 degrees. If not brown enough at end of this time, place under broiler for no more than 5 minutes. Watch closely to avoid overbrowning. Serves 4.

Mrs. M. B. Murray (Lillian)
Cheboygan County (Cheboygan)

SOUFFLÉ BAKED FISH

1½ pounds fish fillets
1 teaspoon salt
¼ teaspoon pepper
2 egg whites
¼ cup mayonnaise
1 tablespoon pickle relish, drained
3 tablespoons scallions, chopped
1 tablespoon parsley, chopped
¼ teaspoon salt
2 drops Tabasco sauce

Preheat oven to 425 degrees. Place fish or frozen and thawed fish fillets in greased baking pan. Sprinkle with salt and pepper. Bake for 10 minutes. In medium-sized bowl, beat egg whites until stiff peaks form. Blend in mayonnaise, drained relish, scallions, parsley, salt and Tabasco. Spread over fish, covering completely. Continue baking for 10 to 15 minutes longer until topping is well puffed and fish flakes easily with fork. Serves 4.

Mrs. Edward L. Twohey (Peg)
Kent County (Grand Rapids)

Fish

SMOKED SALMON OR TROUT

10 pounds salmon or lake trout

2 cups salt
1 cup sugar

Clean fish by cutting and removing head. Cut fish into chunks approximately 1½-inches thick. Soak in brine made of 2 quarts water mixed with sugar and salt for 24 hours. Remove from brine, wash and wipe dry. Build small charcoal fire in middle of Weber grill. Cover fire with soaked green applewood. Arrange fish around outer part of grill and close top, shutting vents. Continue smoking until golden brown.

Fred C. Janke
Jackson County (Jackson)

BAKED CHICKEN BREASTS SUPREME

6 12-ounce broiler-fryer breasts
2 cups dairy sour cream
½ cup lemon juice
4 teaspoons Worcestershire sauce
4 teaspoons celery salt
2 teaspoons paprika

4 cloves garlic, finely chopped
4 teaspoons salt
½ teaspoon pepper
1¾ cups packaged dry bread crumbs
½ cup butter or margarine
½ cup shortening

Cut chicken breasts in ½ and wipe well with damp paper towels. In large bowl, combine sour cream with lemon juice, Worcestershire sauce, celery salt, paprika, garlic, salt and pepper. Add chicken to sour cream mixture, coating each piece well. Let stand, covered in refrigerator overnight. Next day, preheat oven to 350 degrees. Remove chicken from sour cream mixture. Roll in crumbs, coating evenly. Arrange chicken in single layer in large shallow 8x13-inch baking pan. Melt butter and shortening in small saucepan. Spoon ½ over chicken. Bake chicken, uncovered for 45 minutes. Spoon rest of butter mixture over chicken. Bake for 10 to 15 minutes longer or until chicken is tender and nicely browned. *Note: Chicken is marinated overnight. First baking can be done in the morning. Cool chicken quickly and keep in a cool place. Just before serving, bake for 10 to 15 minutes or until chicken is tender and browned.*

Mrs. R. W. Fleming (Sally)
Washtenaw County (Ann Arbor)

AUNT MARY'S BAKED CHICKEN

2 chickens, cut up
¼ cup margarine, melted
3 tablespoons flour
⅛ teaspoon pepper
½ teaspoon paprika

⅛ teaspoon turmeric
1 teaspoon sugar
2 teaspoons salt
¼ cup water

Place the chicken pieces in a large bowl. Melt margarine and pour it over the pieces. Mix flour, pepper, paprika, turmeric, sugar and salt in a small bowl. Sprinkle this mixture on the pieces of chicken and toss well to coat. Place the chicken pieces in an ungreased 13x9-inch pan. Pour the water into the pan. Bake uncovered for 1½ hours or until tender at 300 degrees. Serves 6 to 8.

Mrs. Howard Morrill (Mary)
Presque Isle (Rogers City)

BUSY DAY CHICKEN

1 frying chicken, cut into
  serving size pieces
Salt

Pepper
1 cup catsup
1 cup Coca-Cola

Place chicken pieces in 2-quart casserole and sprinkle with salt and pepper. Mix catsup and Coca-Cola and pour over chicken. Bake in preheated 350 degree oven for 1¼ hours or until chicken is tender.

Blythe Parks
Genesee County (Flint)

CHICKEN DIVINE

1 package frozen chopped
  broccoli, cooked and
  drained
2 cups white meat chicken,
  cooked

2 cans cream of chicken soup
½ cup salad dressing
1 teaspoon lemon juice
10 slices cheese
1 cup bread crumbs

Place drained, cooked broccoli in bottom of greased 13x9-inch pan. Place chicken pieces on top of broccoli. Combine the soup, salad dressing and lemon juice. Pour over chicken. Top with cheese slices and sprinkle with bread crumbs. Bake at 350 degrees for 30 minutes. Serves 6 to 8.

Mrs. Daniel Williams (Jeanne)
Wayne County (Canton)

Poultry

CHICKEN BREASTS, MARIA'S WAY

2 whole chicken breasts, split
Salt and seasoned pepper
¼ cup butter or margarine
¼ cup shallots or green onions, minced
1 clove garlic, minced
1 teaspoon paprika
1 bunch broccoli, freshly cooked and hot
4 cling-peach halves, canned
1 cup dairy sour cream
¼ cup mayonnaise
¼ cup Parmesan or Romano cheese, grated

Season chicken with salt and seasoned pepper. Melt butter in small skillet, add shallots and garlic and sauté a few minutes. Stir in paprika and turn chicken in the mixture until well coated. Put in shallow broiler-proof baking dish and cover loosely with foil. Bake in preheated 375 degree oven for 20 minutes. Arrange well-drained broccoli in pan beside chicken. Put peaches in pan. Mix sour cream and mayonnaise and spoon over all. Sprinkle with the cheese, put low in broiler and broil 6 to 8 minutes, or until glazed and richly flecked with brown. Serves 4.

Mrs. Jerry L. Pinney (Maryjane)
St. Joseph County (Centreville)

CHICKEN CASSEROLE

4 chicken breasts or 8 halves
2 cans Campbell mushroom soup
1 pint sour cream
1 package dry onion soup
1 package Pepperidge Farm Dressing (dry mix)

Cook chicken breasts until done. Cool and cut into bite size pieces. Place in a 9x13-inch baking pan. Combine mushroom soup and sour cream with the dry onion soup mix and pour over chicken. Prepare dry Pepperidge dressing according to package instructions. Sprinkle or spread over top of chicken mixture. Bake at 350 degrees for 1 hour—45 minutes covered and 15 minutes uncovered to brown topping. Serves 6 generously. *Note: This is a good recipe to serve at a hot buffet lunch. If chicken breasts are large, you may have to put a bit in a second casserole.*

Lois M. Stange
Tuscola County (Vassar)

ARTICHOKE CASSEROLE

1 10-ounce can artichoke hearts
2 whole chicken breasts, cooked and diced
⅔ cup Miracle Whip salad dressing
1 10¾-ounce can cream of mushroom soup
1 tablespoon lemon juice
¼ pound butter, melted
1 8-ounce package herbed bread crumbs

Cut artichokes in half and put in the bottom of a casserole dish. Add chicken. Mix salad dressing, soup and lemon juice. Spoon over chicken. Melt butter and stir in bread crumbs. Top casserole with bread crumb mixture. You may have bread crumbs left over. Bake at 350 degrees for 30 minutes. Serve with rice.

Mrs. Lee Luff (Joan)
Marquette County (Marquette)

. . . Rub inside of chicken with lemon juice to sweeten and tenderize.

CHICKEN AND RICE

2 medium onions, chopped
1 cup celery, chopped
1 green pepper, chopped (Optional)
½ cup butter
2 cups long grain rice
Parsley (for color)
6 cups hot chicken broth
1 oven-baked chicken (fryer)
Hot banana peppers (Optional)
Salt, pepper and paprika

Sauté onions, celery and green peppers in butter until soft. Add uncooked rice and parsley and sauté 5 minutes until rice is warmed. Spread this mixture in a casserole or roaster and gently pour 6 cups of hot chicken broth over. Cut up your cooked chicken and place in pan. If you desire a hot dish, place your pierced hot banana peppers in pan. I add salt, pepper, and paprika at this stage on top of the broth. Place in preheated 375 degree oven uncovered and bake about 20 minutes. Center of rice should be soft. *Note: This recipe can be doubled for large groups but be sure to use a pan that the rice will cover completely. I put my banana peppers on one end only and satisfy all my guests.*

Marion Tracy
Oakland County (Franklin)

EASY CHICKEN AND RICE

1 10½-ounce can creamed chicken soup
1 10½-ounce can water
1 cup Minute Rice, uncooked

10 pieces chicken
1 package Lipton onion soup mix
Soy sauce (Optional)

Mix soup and water together. Place rice in a large baking dish and cover with soup and water mixture. Arrange chicken evenly over rice and soup mixture in the baking dish. Sprinkle chicken with onion soup mix. Cover the dish tightly with aluminum foil. Bake at 325 to 350 degrees for 2 hours. Serve in the baking dish and top with soy sauce.

Jo Ann Regis
Montcalm County (Crystal)

EASY HONEY-CURRIED BAKED CHICKEN

1 chicken, ½ chicken or chicken pieces
½ cup mustard

½ cup honey
Curry powder to taste

Place chicken in baking utensil. Mix mustard, honey and curry powder together to make basting sauce. Baste chicken with half of the sauce and use remaining sauce to baste every 15 minutes until chicken is done. Bake at 350 degrees.

Jackie Gordon
Oakland County (Bloomfield Hills)

HOT CHICKEN SALAD

4 cups cooked chicken, diced
2 cups celery, finely cut
1½ cups mayonnaise
1 teaspoon salt
¼ teaspoon Accent
4 hard boiled eggs, chopped

2 tablespoons lemon juice
⅔ cup almonds, chopped
2 pimentos, chopped
1 tablespoon minced onion
2 cups cheese, grated
1½ cups potato chips, crushed

Mix all ingredients except cheese and potato chips together gently. Fold into casserole and top with cheese and crushed potato chips. Bake at 400 degrees for 20 to 25 minutes. Serves 10 to 12. *Note: Good served with cranberry or Jello salad and hot rolls with butter.*

Aneshea Neda
Shiawassee County (Bancroft)

DELICIOUS HOT CHICKEN SALAD

4 cups chicken, chopped and cut in chunks
2 cups celery, chopped
4 hard boiled eggs, sliced
¾ cup mayonnaise
1 cup cream of chcken soup, undiluted
1 small jar pimentos, cut fine
2 teaspoons lemon juice
1 teaspoon onion, minced
1 teaspoon salt
½ teaspoon Accent
1½ cups potato chips, crushed
1 cup cheese, grated
½ cup almonds, chopped

Combine chicken, celery, eggs, soup, mayonnaise, pimentos, lemon juice, onion, salt and Accent. Place in a large greased rectangular baking dish. Top with potato chips, next cheese, then almonds. Cover and refrigerate overnight. Bake in 400 degree oven for 20 to 25 minutes. Serves 8.

Mrs. Leroy Berry
Genesee County (Flint)

DELICIOUS CHICKEN FOR TIMBALES

1 16-ounce can of chicken (or 1 chicken, cooked), boned
3 eggs, hard boiled, quartered or slices
1 cup celery, diced
½ cup ripe olives, sliced
1 cup mushroom soup
¾ cup mayonnaise
½ teaspoon salt
Dash of pepper
1 teaspoon onion, minced
1 tablespoon lemon juice
6 to 8 timbales

Place boned chicken in an 8x12-inch baking dish. Add quartered or sliced eggs. Combine celery and olives and spread evenly over chicken and eggs. Combine mushroom soup, mayonnaise, salt, pepper, onion and lemon juice and pour over casserole. Bake at 400 degrees for 15 minutes. Bake timbales according to package directions. Remove center, fill with chicken mixture and top with rest of timbale shell. Serves 6 to 8. *Note: Recipe can be varied by covering above ingredients with crushed potato chips and eliminating timbales. This recipe has been very popular on Capitol Hill.*

Mrs. Elizabeth Anne Klerk
Kalamazoo County (Kalamazoo)

GOOD-BYE TURKEY CASSEROLE

¾ cups Minute Rice
2 cups cooked turkey
1½ cups cooked asparagus, drained
1⅔ cups chicken broth

Dash of onion or garlic salt
1 can cream of chicken soup
½ cup American cheese, grated
2 tablespoons slivered almonds

Grease a 2-quart casserole dish. Mix the above ingredients and pour into greased casserole. Top with buttered bread crumbs if desired. Bake at 375 degrees for 1 hour (45 minutes covered and 15 minutes uncovered). *Note: I use 1 cup of bread dressing and leftover gravy in this if I have it.*

Thelma Conklin
Clinton County (Elsie)

TURKEY "THE INSIDE STORY"

When planning to buy a turkey, figure about ¾ to 1 pound per person for turkeys 12 pounds or under. About ½ to ¾ pound per person when buying a larger bird. Defrosting a 12 pound turkey takes about 3 to 4 days in the refrigerator and about 4 to 5 days for 16 pounds. Roasting time varies with each turkey, but the approximate time for stuffed birds is:

6 to 8   pounds at 325 degrees = 2 to 2½ hours
8 to 12 pounds at 325 degrees = 2½ to 3 hours
12 to 16 pounds at 325 degrees = 3 to 3¾ hours
16 to 20 pounds at 325 degrees = 3¾ to 4½ hours
20 to 24 pounds at 325 degrees = 4½ to 5½ hours

Rinse bird inside and out, drain and pat dry. Rub skin lightly with salt. Stuff neck cavity, fasten with a skewer. Stuff body cavity loosely and close with skewers or with needle and thread. Fold wings back and tie legs to tail with string. Roast, basting with pan juices several times. *Note: When using a thermometer, bring temperature to 170 degrees and allow to stand 15 minutes before cooling.*

Lillian Brinker, Gourmet teacher
Oakland County (Rochester)

Entrees

Entrees

SUNDAY BRUNCH QUICHE

1 pound pork sausage
1 onion, finely chopped
½ pound Swiss cheese, grated
1 tablespoon flour
1 9-inch pie shell, unbaked
4 eggs, lightly beaten
1½ cups light cream
½ teaspoon salt
¼ teaspoon pepper
¼ teaspoon grated nutmeg
2 tablespoons chopped parsley
½ teaspoon crumbled dry leaf sage

Preheat oven to 375 degrees. Brown sausage in frying pan until crisp, stirring occasionally to separate. Remove sausage and drain on paper towel. Heat 2 tablespoons of sausage drippings and sauté onion until tender. Set aside. Place cheese in bowl and sprinkle with flour and toss. Sprinkle sausage over bottom of pie shell, reserve 1 cup. Sprinkle onion and cheese over sausage. Place egg, cream, salt, pepper, nutmeg, parsley and sage in electric blender and blend at low speed until mixed. Pour egg over sausage, onion and cheese and sprinkle with reserved sausage. Bake for 35 to 40 minutes or until silver knife, stuck in middle remains clean. Yield: 4 servings.

Marilyn Turner
WXYZ-TV Detroit
Cookbook Chairperson

SPINACH QUICHE

16 slices bacon, fried and crumbled
2 9-inch pastry shells, unbaked
2 large onions, thinly sliced
12 ounces Swiss cheese, grated
Salt and pepper to taste
1¼ cups spinach, cooked, chopped and well-drained
6 eggs, well beaten
3 cups Half and Half

Sprinkle well-drained bacon crumbs in unbaked pastry shell. Sauté onions and place over bacon. Sprinkle grated cheese over onion layer, add layer of spinach. (Be sure you squeeze spinach to extract all the water.) Beat eggs with Half and Half and season with salt and pepper. Pour over pie. Bake at 450 degrees for 10 minutes, then reduce heat to 300 degrees and bake an additional 45 minutes or until custard sets. Serves 10.

Edna Schuur
Kalamazoo County (Kalamazoo)

CHEESE CROQUETTES

4 tablespoons butter
5 tablespoons flour
1½ cups milk
Salt and pepper to taste

½ pound Switzerland Swiss
    cheese, grated
3 egg yolks, beaten

Melt butter over low heat, add flour and stir until golden colored. Add milk and stir until smooth. Cook slowly for about 10 minutes, stirring constantly. Add salt and pepper and remove from heat. Add cheese, stir until dissolved. Add egg yolks and stir well. Spread mixture on well-buttered pan to cool. When cool, cover with Handi-Wrap and refrigerate 2 hours until firm. Form croquette in the shape of a sausage or small frank.

Batter:
1 egg
¼ cup milk
1 tablespoon oil

Dish of flour
Dish of fine bread crumbs

Beat egg with milk and oil. Roll each croquette in flour, dip into the egg mixture, and then cover completely in bread crumbs. Fry in deep fat at 375 degrees (if oil is too hot, croquettes will split). Serve with your favorite tomato sauce. *Note: These classic croquettes are a great favorite with everyone, served with a vegetable and green salad and fruit for dessert. They are also terrific as an appetizer, rolled to bite-size and dipped in a hot tomato sauce or a mustard sauce. They can be made in quantity and frozen before frying. Remember: The quality of the cheese makes a big difference in the results.*

Mrs. Donald H. Freeman
Kent County (Grand Rapids)

MACARONI CASSEROLE

2 cups macaroni, uncooked
4 hard-boiled eggs, coarsely
    chopped
2 cans cream of mushroom
    soup

1 pint milk
1½ teaspoons salt
2 teaspoons onion, finely cut
1 3-ounce package dried beef
¼ cup Cheddar cheese, shredded

In large casserole dish combine macaroni, eggs, soup, milk, salt, onion dried beef and cheese. Mix well and refrigerate all night or all day before baking. Bake at 350 degrees for 1 hour. Serves 8.

Gertrude Webb
Alcona County (Lincoln)

Entrees

CHEESE RAREBIT

2 tablespoons flour
½ stick margarine
16 ounces tomato juice

½ pound sharp processed cheese, grated

Mix flour and margarine in saucepan over low heat until smooth. Slowly add tomato juice until hot and thickened. Stir in cheese. Serve over warmed soda crackers or toast points. Serves 4 for luncheon. *Note: May add shrimp or crabmeat just before serving if desired.*

Doris A. Lindsay
Cheboygan County (Cheboygan)

CRAZY CRUST PIE

Crust:
½ cup flour
½ cup sour cream
¼ cup shortening

1 egg
½ teaspoon salt
½ teaspoon baking powder

Combine all ingredients. Batter will be lumpy. Press into greased 9-inch pie dish. Spread batter thin on the bottom and thick on the sides to ¼ inch from rim of dish. Note: Quiche dish works well also.

Filling:
1½ pounds hamburger
1 teaspoon salt
1 teaspoon oregano
1 teaspoon sweet basil
½ teaspoon garlic powder
¼ cup onions, chopped

1 6-ounce can tomato paste
1 4-ounce can mushrooms, undrained
4 ounces Mozzarella cheese, shredded

Brown hamburger and drain well. Add all ingredients except Mozzarella cheese. Mix well. Pour into crust batter. Bake at 350 degrees for 20 to 25 minutes. Before serving, sprinkle cheese on top and put back in oven until cheese melts. Serves 4.

Mary Szymanski
Otsego County (Gaylord)

PIZZA CASSEROLE

1 large onion, chopped
3 to 4 stalks celery, chopped
1 green pepper, chopped
1½ pounds ground beef
2 10-ounce cans pizza sauce
1 16-ounce can tomatoes
1 teaspoon salt
½ teaspoon garlic powder
½ teaspoon oregano
1 8-ounce bag medium-width noodles
1 cup (about 4 ounces) Cheddar cheese, grated
1 cup (about 4 ounces) Mozzarella cheese, grated

Chop onion, celery and green pepper and set aside. Begin browning ground beef in large skillet adding the chopped onion, celery and green pepper when the meat is nearly browned. Cook together until meat is brown and vegetables are softened. Add pizza sauce, tomatoes and spices to skillet mixture and stir to mix well. Cook noodles according to package directions in boiling water. Drain noodles and pour into ungreased 9x13-inch baking pan. Slowly pour hot mixture over noodles and stir carefully to mix. Sprinkle cheeses alternately over top of casserole. Bake at 325 degrees for 45 to 50 minutes. Serve in pan to 6 to 8 people.

Mrs. Max Tate (Patricia)
Oceana County (Shelby)

SPAGHETTI PIE

7 to 8 ounces spaghetti, uncooked
1 cup cottage cheese
2 eggs, slightly beaten
1 cup Cheddar cheese, grated
1 teaspoon salt
¼ teaspoon basil
1 egg, beaten
2 tablespoons Parmesan cheese, grated

Cook spaghetti according to package directions, then drain. Combine spaghetti with cottage cheese, 2 eggs, salt, basil and Cheddar cheese. Place in a buttered 9-inch pie plate. Top with a mixture of 1 egg and Parmesan cheese. Bake for 45 to 50 minutes or until silver knife inserted in center comes out clean. Cut in pie-shaped wedges and serve with mushroom or tomato soup.

Mrs. Larry Yeagley (Roberta)
Calhoun County (Battle Creek)

Entrees

DELICIOUS SPAGHETTI PIE

1 6-ounce package spaghetti
2 tablespoons butter
⅓ cup Parmesan cheese, grated
2 eggs, well beaten
1½ pounds ground beef
1 cup onion, chopped
¼ cup green pepper, chopped
1 8-ounce can tomatoes, cut up
1 6-ounce can tomato paste
1 teaspoon sugar
1 teaspoon dried oregano
1 teaspoon garlic salt (Optional)
1 cup cottage cheese
½ cup Mozzarella cheese, shredded

Cook spaghetti according to package directions and drain. There should be about 3¼ cups spaghetti. Stir in butter, Parmesan cheese and eggs. Form into a crust in a 10-inch buttered pie plate. In skillet, cook ground beef, onion and green pepper until vegetables are tender and meat is browned. Drain off excess fat. Stir in undrained tomatoes, tomato paste, sugar, oregano and garlic salt. Heat thoroughly. Spread cottage cheese over bottom of spaghetti crust and fill pie with tomato-meat mixture. Bake uncovered in 350 degree oven for 20 minutes. Sprinkle with Mozzarella cheese and bake 5 minutes longer or until cheese melts. Serves 8 to 10.

Marilyn Olson
Delta County (Gladstone)

SATURDAY SPECIAL

1 4-ounce package dried beef
3 tablespoons margarine
½ cup onion, chopped
⅓ cup celery, diagonally sliced
2 1-pound cans pork and beans with tomato sauce
1 tablespoon Worcestershire sauce
¼ cup Cheddar cheese, shredded

Rinse dried beef with boiling water and shred. Brown beef in margarine in a saucepan and cook onion and celery until tender. Add beans and Worcestershire sauce to mixture. Pour into a 1½-quart casserole and bake at 350 degrees for 40 minutes. Top with Cheddar cheese and bake 5 minutes longer. Serve with hot corn bread. Serves 4 to 6.

Hazel S. Adams
Oakland County (Novi)

CALIFORNIA STYLE ITALIAN SPAGHETTI SAUCE WITH MEATBALLS

Meatballs:
1½ pounds ground round or chuck
½ pound ground pork or Italian sausage
2 eggs
½ teaspoon oregano, chopped
½ tablespoon garlic, chopped
½ cup onions, chopped
1 cup bread crumbs
1 tablespoon parsley, finely chopped
⅛ teaspoon black pepper, ground

Mix all ingredients well. Shape into meatballs. Place in 1 or 2-inch deep pan and brown well by roasting in 375 degree oven. When browned, remove from oven.

Sauce:
3 ounces olive oil
½ cup onions, chopped
½ tablespoon garlic, chopped
2 29-ounce cans crushed tomatoes
2 29-ounce cans tomato sauce
1 6-ounce can tomato paste
15 ounces water
½ teaspoon oregano, chopped
⅛ teaspoon black pepper
2 bay leaves
Salt to taste
1 to 2 tablespoons sugar
¼ cup Parmesan cheese, grated

Pour olive oil into a 4 or 5-quart pressure cooker without top or a heavy cast aluminum pot. Add chopped onions and garlic and allow to simmer and brown. Immediately add tomatoes, tomato sauce and tomato paste, stirring well. Add approximately 15 ounces of water. Add oregano, ground pepper, bay leaves and salt to taste. Stir well for 15 to 20 minutes using medium to medium-low heat. Allow to simmer at least 4 to 5 hours adding water as needed. Add sugar to reduce acidity of tomatoes. Add Parmesan cheese. Stir well. Allow to simmer until ready to serve on: spaghetti, pasta, noodles or corn meal mush. Serves 8 to 12.

Dr. Louis C. Vaccaro
Lenawee County (Adrian)

. . . Add 1 slice of crumbled bread and a little water to 1 pound ground beef for soft and moist hamburgers.

Entrees

HAMBURGER PIE

2 cups flour
¾ cup instant mashed potato granules
1 tablespoon sugar
1 teaspoon Cream of Tartar
1 teaspoon soda
8 tablespoons margarine
½ cup milk
¼ cup mayonnaise
4 ounces Cheddar cheese, shredded

1 pound ground beef
½ cup onion, chopped
1 egg, beaten
¼ cup catsup
1 tablespoon sweet pickle relish
1 teaspoon prepared mustard
¾ teaspoon salt
⅛ teaspoon pepper

Mix flour, ¼ cup potato granules, sugar, Cream of Tartar and soda. Cut in 6 tablespoons of margarine until mixture resembles coarse crumbs. Add milk and mayonnaise. Stir until moistened. On floured surface, roll a little over half of the dough to fit a 9-inch pie plate. Fit in place and sprinkle half the cheese over the crust. Cook the ground beef and onions. Drain and stir in ¼ cup potato granules, egg, catsup, relish, mustard, salt and pepper. Spread over cheese in crust. Sprinkle rest of cheese over meat mixture. Roll out remaining dough and adjust over pie. Trim, seal and flute edges. Mix remaining potato granules and 2 tablespoons melted margarine. Sprinkle over top of pie. Bake at 350 degrees for 35 to 40 minutes. Serves 6.

Maxine Ropp
St. Joseph County (Sturgis)

PORCUPINE BALLS

1 pound ground beef
½ cup uncooked rice
2 tablespoons green pepper, chopped
1 tablespoon onion, chopped

¼ teaspoon black pepper
1½ teaspoons salt
1 small can tomato soup
1 cup water
2 tablespoons fat, melted

Blend beef, rice, green pepper, onion, pepper and salt together thoroughly. Shape into balls in large heavy skillet. Pour tomato soup, water and melted fat over meatballs. Cook over high heat until steaming, then turn to low heat for 45 minutes. Serves 6.

Jeanne Lee
Kalkaska County (Kalkaska)

BARBECUED SPARERIBS

3 to 4 pounds country ribs, cut into pieces
2 lemons, sliced
2 onions, sliced
1 cup catsup
⅓ cup Worcestershire sauce
1 teaspoon chili powder
1 teaspoon salt
2 dashes Tabasco sauce
2 cups water

Place ribs in shallow roasting pan, meaty side up. Place a slice of lemon and a slice of onion on each piece of meat. Secure with toothpick and roast in 450 degree oven for 30 minutes. Combine catsup, Worcestershire sauce, chili powder, salt, Tabasco, and water in saucepan and bring to boil. Pour this mixture over ribs. Continue baking ribs in 350 degree oven until tender—about 1½ hours. Baste ribs every 15 minutes.

Jean P. Clime
Cass County (Marcellus)

... To retain juices in meat, thaw in refrigerator.

BARBARA'S BARBECUED SPARERIBS

4 pounds spareribs
1 clove garlic
1 large onion, diced
2 tablespoons butter
1 cup canned tomatoes
1 cup green pepper, diced
1 cup celery, diced
1 cup catsup
2 tablespoons brown sugar
3 dashes Tabasco sauce
½ teaspoon dry mustard
2 cups beef stock or 2 bouillon cubes dissolved in 2 cups boiling water
Salt and pepper to taste

Rub ribs with cut side of garlic clove. Place in shallow baking pan; roast uncovered at 350 degrees for 30 minutes. Meanwhile, brown onion in melted butter in heavy fry pan. Add remaining ingredients. Stir and cover. Simmer over low heat for 1 hour. After ribs have roasted the 30 minutes, pour sauce over them. Roast 45 minutes longer, basting frequently. Serves 4.

Mrs. C. Glen Catt (Barbara)
Otsego County (Gaylord)

Entrees

FLANK STEAK PINWHEELS

2 flank steaks
1 pound bacon

Salt and pepper

Cook bacon until almost done, but not crisp. Sprinkle flank steak with salt and pepper. Pound lightly and score steak diagonally on both sides making diamond-shaped cuts. Slice lengthwise into 1-inch wide long strips. Place a piece of bacon on each steak strip. Roll pinwheel fashion and secure with toothpicks. Arrange in 8x12-inch glass baking dish. Pour marinade over pinwheels and marinate overnight. Remove pinwheels from marinade and grill to desired doneness. Yield: Approximately 10 pinwheels.

Marinade:
1 cup catsup
1 teaspoon salt
4 tablespoons A-1 Sauce
4 tablespoons white sugar
4 tablespoons vinegar

4 tablespoons Worcestershire sauce
4 tablespoons vegetable oil
½ cup water

Combine all marinade ingredients and heat to boil. *Note: Marinade may be reheated and served as sauce with pinwheels.*

Mrs. Jack Van Eden (Marcia)
Ottawa County (Zeeland)

ITALIAN BREADED STEAK

3 pounds sirloin steak (or tenderized round steak)
1½ cups cooking oil

1½ cups Italian style seasoned bread crumbs

Cut steak into serving pieces. Dip both sides of steak in oil and bread crumbs. Place on rack until coating is completely dry and repeat coating process. (This will insure uniform coating of steak.) Place steak on broiler pan and broil until steak reaches desired tenderness. Serves 4.

Linda LaFaive
Emmet County (Harbor Springs)

BAVARIAN POT ROAST

3 to 4 pound beef chuck roast
2 tablespoons shortening
Salt and pepper to taste
2 8-ounce cans tomato sauce
1 tablespoon vinegar
2 tablespoons sugar

1 teaspoon salt
1 teaspoon cinnamon
½ teaspoon ginger
1 bay leaf (Optional)
⅔ cup onion, chopped

Brown meat in hot shortening. Drain excess fat and season meat to taste with salt and pepper. Combine tomato sauce, vinegar, sugar, salt, cinnamon, ginger, bay leaf and onion and mix well. Pour over meat. Cover tightly and bake in a preheated 350 degree oven for 2½ to 3 hours or until meat is tender. If necessary, skim fat from sauce and serve sauce over meat. Serves 6 to 8.

Mrs. Rachel Musselman
Gratiot County (St. Louis)

. . . Use wine and tomatoes to break down the tough fiber in meat.

ITALIAN POT ROAST

3 to 4 pound chuck roast
1 quart stewed tomatoes
1 package dry onion soup mix
1 teaspoon oregano
2 tablespoons wine

2 tablespoons vinegar
2 tablespoons oil
¼ teaspoon cracked pepper
⅛ teaspoon garlic powder

Cut roast into serving size pieces. Place in large frying pan and add tomatoes, onion soup mix, oregano, wine, vinegar, oil, pepper and garlic powder. Simmer for 2 hours. *Note: If you substitute round steak or chuck steak for chuck roast simmer for 1½ hours. You can also substitute ¼ cup wine vinegar for wine and vinegar.*

Mrs. John Brancaleon (Joyce)
Cass County (Cassopolis)

Entrees

TOMATO BEEF OVER RICE

1 pound stew beef, cubed
1 large onion, chopped
2 green peppers, chopped
1 10½-ounce can tomato
   soup
2 2-pound cans tomatoes
½ cup red cooking wine
4 beef bouillon cubes
1 teaspoon salt
½ teaspoon pepper
2 tablespoons sugar
Cornstarch
½ cup water
4 cups rice, hot cooked

Place stew beef in large saucepan. Add chopped onion and green peppers to the beef. Stir in tomato soup, tomatoes, red wine, and bouillon cubes. Add sugar, salt and pepper. Bring mixture to boil and then simmer covered for 1½ hours. Blend cornstarch and ½ cup water. Gradually stir the cornstarch into the tomato mixture and boil until thickened. Serve over hot cooked rice. *Note: Add soy sauce for a nice oriental flavor.*

Jacquolyn Mitchell
Washtenaw County (Ann Arbor)

BEEF BURGUNDY

2 pounds beef round steak, cut
   in ¼-inch pieces
¼ cup all-purpose flour
¼ cup butter or margarine
½ cup onion, coarsely
   chopped
1 tablespoon parsley, finely
   snipped
1 medium clove garlic, crushed
1 teaspoon salt
Dash freshly ground pepper
1 8-ounce can whole mushrooms,
   drained
1 cup burgundy wine
½ cup water

Cut steak into bite-size pieces; coat with flour. In 12-inch skillet, quickly brown on both sides in butter. Remove from heat. Add onion, parsley, garlic, salt and a dash of freshly ground pepper. Stir in mushrooms, wine and ½ cup water. Bring to a boil reduce heat; simmer covered for 1 hour or until tender. Add more water during cooking if necessary. Serve over rice. Serves 6.

Mrs. Lee Brayton (Jean)
Branch County (Coldwater)

REUBEN BAKE

1 8-ounce package egg noodles
2 tablespoons butter
1 16-ounce can sauerkraut
1 12-ounce can corned beef
½ cup Miracle Whip salad dressing
2 cups Swiss cheese, shredded
1 large tomato, sliced
½ cup cracker crumbs
¼ teaspoon caraway seeds
2 tablespoons butter

Cook noodles as directed on package. Place cooked noodles in a 12x9-inch cake pan. Toss noodles with butter. Spread sauerkraut over noodles, then cover with shredded corned beef, Miracle Whip, tomato, and Swiss cheese. Melt butter and toss with cracker crumbs and caraway seeds. Sprinkle crumb mixture over cheese. Bake until hot and bubbly in 350 degree oven for about 1 hour. Serves 6 to 8.

Mrs. Matthew Sherock (Edith)
Iosco County (Hale)

GRILLED LEG OF LAMB

1¼ pounds butter
5 cloves garlic
½ cup onions, diced
1 cup mint leaves, minced
¼ ounce vinegar
1 leg of lamb, boned

Melt butter and mix with garlic, onions, mint leaves and vinegar. Ask butcher to bone leg of lamb and butterfly. Leg of lamb will now look like a sirloin steak. Prepare grill as you would to grill a steak outdoors. Pour mint mixture over lamb 20 minutes before grilling lamb. Save mixture and baste lamb from time to time while grilling. Grill 12 minutes for rare and 15 minutes for medium. Slice and serve with honey sauce. *Note: Lamb can also be grilled in your oven under the broiler.*

Honey Sauce:
1 cup honey
Juice of 3 lemons
2 teaspoons salt
½ tablespoon garlic salt
1 cup Dijon mustard

Combine all ingredients and set aside to serve at table with grilled lamb.

Mr. Ernest A. Jones II (Biff)
St. Louis, Missouri

HAM AND POTATO SKILLET

1 1-pound slice ready-to-eat ham
1 tablespoon butter
1 tablespoon brown sugar
1 can cream of mushroom soup
⅔ cup Pet evaporated milk (small can)
⅓ cup water
¼ cup onion, coarsely chopped
½ teaspoon salt
⅛ teaspoon pepper
3 cups raw potatoes, peeled and thinly sliced
1 cup raw carrots, sliced

In 10-inch skillet, brown ham slice in butter and brown sugar. Remove ham and pour off drippings. Mix in same skillet, soup, milk, water, onion, salt and pepper. Stir in potatoes and carrots. Cover and cook over low heat stirring now and then, until vegetables are tender (about 35 minutes). Place ham on vegetables. Cover and cook about 10 minutes longer. Serves 4.

Mrs. O. E. Spencer (Dorinda)
Emmet County (Petoskey)

BLENDER-OVEN CATSUP

48 medium tomatoes (about 8 pounds)
2 ripe sweet red peppers
2 sweet green peppers
4 medium onions, peeled and quartered
3 cups vinegar
3 cups sugar
3 tablespoons salt
1½ teaspoons allspice
3 teaspoons dry mustard
1½ teaspoons cloves
1½ teaspoons cinnamon
½ teaspoon red hot pepper sauce

Quarter tomatoes; remove stem ends, add peppers, seeded and cut in strips, and onions. Mix together well. Put vegetables in blender, filling container ¾ full. Blend at high speed 4 seconds; pour into large roaster. Repeat until all vegetables are blended. Add vinegar, sugar, salt, spices and pepper sauce. Simmer uncovered in 325 degree oven until volume is reduced in half. Seal immediately in hot sterilized 1 pint canning jars. Process 15 minutes in hot water. Yield: 5 pints. *Note: Makes very thick catsup the easy, quick way.*

Eleanor L. Thornton
Shiawassee County (Owosso)

INDIAN CHILI SAUCE

12 sour apples, cored, peeled, and sliced
12 ripe tomatoes, peeled and cored
9 large onions, finely chopped
1 quart vinegar
3 cups sugar
¼ cup salt
1 teaspoon pepper
1 teaspoon ginger
1 teaspoon cinnamon
1 teaspoon dry mustard
1 teaspoon cloves

Combine all ingredients in large kettle and boil for 1½ hours. Can in sterile glass jars. Yield: Approximately 9 pints.

Lori I. Hughes
Bay County (Essexville)

BARBECUE SAUCE

¼ cup salad oil
1 8-ounce can tomato sauce
½ cup water
¼ cup brown sugar
¼ cup lemon juice
3 tablespoons Worcestershire sauce
2 teaspoons mustard
2 teaspoons salt
¼ teaspoon pepper
1 cup onions, chopped

Mix together all of the above ingredients, adding onions last. Simmer for at least 1 hour, covered for the first 30 minutes and uncovered the second 30 minutes. *Note: Delicious over an English cut roast that has been prepared on the grill or in the oven. Great over a pork roast or chops. Prepare a double recipe and keep in freezer for those unexpected guests or a rush dinner.*

Dawn Downing
Gladwin County (Beaverton)

SAUSAGE SOUFFLE

6 slices white bread
1 package Brown and Serve sausage
1 cup sharp cheese, grated
4 eggs, beaten
2 cups milk
½ teaspoon salt
1 teaspoon dry mustard

Cube bread, removing crust. Cut sausage into small pieces and brown. In a greased casserole or pan, place a layer of bread. Cover with a layer of sausage and then a layer of cheese. Repeat with a second layer of bread, sausage and cheese. Beat eggs. Add milk and seasonings. Pour over bread. Cover and let stand in refrigerator overnight. Remove cover and bake for 1 hour at 325 degrees. Serve immediately.

Mrs. Tony Fittante (Pat)
Delta County (Escanaba)

FLOSSIE'S COMPANY PORK CHOPS

4 1¼-inch thick pork chops
1 cup uncooked rice
½ cup water
4 ½-inch thick Bermuda onion slices

1 15-ounce can Hunt's tomato sauce

Brown pork chops on both sides and put in Dutch oven that has a tight cover. Bring rice and water to a hard boil in a saucepan. Remove from fire and let stand while you prepare the onion slices. Place 1 onion slice on each pork chop. Divide the rice in 4 sections and place on top of the onion on each pork chop. The rice should mold into a ball shape. Pour can of tomato sauce over each pork chop until sauce is gone. Cover and bake at 350 degrees for 1½ hours. Serves 4.

Lila Baldwin Kline
Kalkaska County (Kalkaska)

BAKED PORK CHOPS WITH APPLES

8 pork chops
Garlic salt to taste
4 tablespoons butter
3 medium apples, peeled and chopped

1 medium onion, chopped
2 cans condensed cream of celery soup
2 cups light cream

Arrange pork chops in a shallow baking dish. Season with garlic salt. Saute apples and onions in butter until transparent. Add soup and cream to this mixture and stir until smooth. Pour sauce over pork chops and bake for 1½ hours at 350 degrees.

Mrs. Fred Graczyk (Diane)
Oakland County (Orchard Lake)

This section was
made possible by a
gift from Hiram Walker, Inc.

International Collection

BOILED KIELBASA AND KRAUT

4 to 5 medium whole potatoes
3 to 4 whole onions
4 to 5 cloves garlic, peeled
1½ pounds fresh kraut

3 pounds kielbasa
1 teaspoon oregano
1 teaspoon crushed red pepper
2 teaspoons black pepper

Put potatoes, onions and garlic in 2 quarts water. Boil for 20 minutes. Add kraut, kielbasa, seasonings and boil at low heat for additional 30 minutes. Should be ready to serve. *Note: The Kielbasa and Kraut is a favorite of mine because it is a complete meal and can be stored and reheated indefinitely. Best served with corn bread and buttermilk.*

Coleman A. Young
Mayor of Detroit
Wayne County (Detroit)

. . . Grease pitcher spout with butter or margarine to prevent dripping.

AFRICAN CHALMAGNE

1½ pounds veal or lean pork, cubed
1 medium onion, diced
¾ cup raw rice
1 can cream of chicken soup

1 can cream of mushroom soup
2 soup cans water
3 tablespoons soy sauce
1 cup celery, diced

Brown meat and onions. Season with salt and pepper. Add remaining ingredients and place in buttered casserole. Bake at 350 degrees for 1½ hours. Keep covered for first hour and then remove cover for last half hour for browning. Serves 6 to 8.

Bonnie Dalman
Osceola County (Reed City)

PHILIPPINE PANSIT BIHON

2 ounces bean threads
½ pound bihon (rice sticks)
3 eggs
¼ teaspoon salt
2¼ teaspoons monosodium glutamate, divided
2 tablespoons oil, divided
1 tablespoon garlic, crushed
½ cup oil
1 onion, sliced
1 cup chicken or Vegeburger, cooked and diced
1 tablespoon black dried mushrooms, soaked and drained
1 cup warm water
1¼ teaspoons salt
1 teaspoon garlic powder
Dash pepper
1½ cups carrots, cut in 1-inch strips
2 cups mushrooms, sliced
2 cups French cut green beans
4 cups cabbage, shreddded
2 cups celery, sliced
1 tablespoon soy sauce
1 cup roasted peanuts, chopped
1 lemon, cut in small wedges

Soak bean threads and rice sticks in warm water for 5 minutes. Drain. Beat eggs with ¼ teaspoon salt and ¼ teaspoon monosodium glutamate. Heat 1 tablespoon oil in frying pan. Pour ½ of the egg mixture, rotating quickly to cover bottom of pan. Cook until golden brown. Repeat for the remaining ½ of the egg mixture. Cut into strips and set aside. Brown garlic and set aside. Heat oil in a big wok or skillet. Sauté onion, chicken or meat substitute and black mushrooms for 2 minutes. Add water, salt, 1 teaspoon monosodium glutamate, garlic powder and pepper. Simmer 2 more minutes. Add carrots, mushrooms and green beans. When vegetables are ½ done, reduce heat to medium and mix in bean threads. Simmer 1 minute then add cabbage and celery. Place the bihon noodles on top of the hot vegetable mixture. Sprinkle soy sauce and 1 teaspoon monosodium glutamate on the cold bihon. Gently work the soy sauce into the noodles until noodles are uniformly colored by the soy sauce. Mix the noodles with the hot mixture. Reduce to low heat, cover and cook 5 minutes, stirring occasionally. Add chopped peanuts, browned crushed garlic and egg strips. Serve with lemon. Serves 10 to 15. *Note: Substitute spaghettini or vermicelli if rice sticks are not available.*

Mrs. Demetrio M. Hechanova (Fidela)
Berrien County (Berrien Springs)

. . . Add 1 teaspoon of vinegar to 1 cup of sweet milk to make sour milk for cooking.

International

KIBBI

- 1 pound lean lamb, finely ground (from leg or shoulder)
- 1 teaspoon salt
- 1 small onion, finely chopped
- ⅓ pound fine bulgar (steamed cracker wheat)
- ½ teaspoon salt
- ½ teaspoon pepper
- 2 tablespoons butter
- ½ cup onion, chopped
- ½ pound lean lamb, finely diced
- 2 tablespoons fine nuts
- ½ cup butter, melted

Combine finely ground lamb with salt and chopped onions. Knead with hands and set aside. Soak bulgar in lukewarm water to cover for 10 minutes. Rinse under running water. Add salt and pepper. Combine with hands, then blend in Cuisinart in small batches until pasty. Meanwhile, melt 2 tablespoons butter in skillet. Add chopped onion and glaze. Add diced lamb and brown. Stir in fine nuts. Melt ½ cup butter and pour enough in a 9x11-inch pan to cover bottom and sides. Spread ½ of ground meat mixture in pan. Press in firmly. Spread diced lamb mixture over this. Cover with remaining ground meat and press firmly all over. Cut into small squares. Separate a bit with a spatula. Pour remaining butter over the top. Bake at 400 degrees for 45 minutes or until cooked through and browned. Separate the squares. Serve hot or cold. Accompany with Eggplant Caviar and plain yogurt.

Eggplant Caviar:
- 1 medium eggplant
- 1 medium onion, quartered
- 1 clove garlic
- 2 tablespoons minced parsley
- 1 teaspoon sugar
- 3 tablespoons olive oil
- 2 tablespoons lemon juice
- 1 tomato, peeled, seeded, squeezed dry and coarsely chopped
- Salt and pepper to taste

Cook whole eggplant in simmering water to cover until tender (approximately 20 to 25 minutes). Cool and peel. Place onion, garlic and parsley in Cuisinart and chop. Add eggplant pulp and blend thoroughly. Add sugar, olive oil, lemon juice, tomato and parsley. Turn on and off a couple of times to blend. Add salt and pepper to taste. Chill mixture well. Serve with Kibbi or with rye bread or Melba Toast Rounds.

Marcia Sikarskie, Cooking Instructor
Washtenaw County (Ann Arbor)

ZUPPA STRACCIATELLA CON SPINACI

6 cups chicken broth
3 eggs
¼ teaspoon salt
Freshly grated nutmeg
3 tablespoons fine bread crumbs
¼ cup Parmesan cheese, freshly grated
½ pound spinach, cooked and chopped

In a 3 quart pan, bring 5 cups of broth to a boil. Beat together eggs, salt, nutmeg, bread crumbs, Parmesan cheese and 1 cup of broth. Whisk this mixture into the boiling broth. Add the spinach and cook 1 minute. Correct seasonings.

Nell Benedict, Director
Continental Cuisine School of Cooking
Oakland County (Royal Oak)

... Add a few drops of ammonia to clean greasy dishes.

CHICKEN FRICASSEE

2 chickens, disjointed
Salt and pepper
Flour
2 tablespoons butter
2 tablespoons oil
2 large onions, chopped
2 cloves garlic, minced
1½ cups mushrooms, sliced
2 tomatoes, peeled and diced
¼ pound ground beef, cooked
1 teaspoon tomato paste
½ teaspoon BV or meat glaze
½ cup dry white wine
2 cups good chicken stock
2 teaspoons potato flour
1 teaspoon apricot jam

Season chicken with salt and pepper. Dredge in flour and shake off excess. Sauté slowly in fat and oil until golden brown. Remove chickens from pan and place in a casserole. Pour out most of the oil leaving approximately 2 tablespoons. Add onions and sauté several minutes. Add garlic and mushrooms and sauté a few minutes more. Add tomatoes and beef. Stir and add tomato paste and meat glaze and mix thoroughly. Pour in wine, chicken broth, and potato flour; simmer a few minutes and add jam. Correct seasoning with salt (up to 1 teaspoon more) and pepper. Serves 6.

Helen Wachler, Cooking Instructor
Oakland County (Farmington Hills)

SWEDISH CHRISTMAS SAUSAGE
(Korv)

6 yards hog casings
Salt
Water
2 cups mashed potatoes, not seasoned
3 medium onions, finely chopped
3 pounds lean beef and 3 pounds lean pork, ground together
2 teaspoons ground allspice

3 tablespoons salt
1 tablespoon ground pepper (seasoned pepper is good)
Pinch bay leaves, chopped
Pinch oregano
Pinch powdered cloves
2½ cups beef or pork stock (or 2½ cups scalded milk, cooled)
Crisco
½ cup water

Items Needed Before Beginning:
Kitchen grinder with spout or sausage machine

Scissors
Heavy thread or light twine

Get hog casings from your butcher. You may need to order them ahead of time. Pick up casings the day before you make the sausage and soak them overnight in a mild salt brine in your refrigerator. Rinse with cold water before using. Make mashed potatoes (packaged are fine). Chop onions finely and sauté in a little Crisco. Do not let brown. Cool. Mix very thoroughly meat, mashed potatoes, onions, allspice, salt, pepper, bay leaves, oregano, powdered cloves and stock. Put a little vegetable oil on spout of grinder or sausage machine. Fry a pinch of mixture in Crisco to test the flavor. Add more seasonings if you need them. Flavor of allspice is important but should be subtle. Mixture should be light. Add more stock if needed. Rinse casings in cold water and cut into 16-inch pieces (approximately). Tie one end of each section. Fill grinder or sausage machine with meat mixture. Ease end of casing (about 2 inches) onto spout. Turn handle slowly. Stop turning 1½ inches from end of casing. Don't pack sausage casing too tightly. Remove from spout and tie second end. Put in Baggies and freeze or refrigerate in a mild salt brine with saltpeter not more than 4 or 5 days. To cook, defrost and set oven at 250 degrees. In an open shallow pan, put 2 tablespoons of Crisco and ½ cup water (or just ½ cup of water). Place sausages in pan and cook for 45 minutes. Turn once to brown evenly. At the end of 45 minutes, if not completely browned, turn heat to 350 degrees, but watch sausages so as not to burn them. For dinner, cut in 1½ inch pieces. Serve warm. A side dish of cranberries goes well. They are great as one dish for a buffet. For hors d'oeuvres, cut in ½ inch pieces and serve warm using cocktail picks.

(Recipe continued on next page)

Variations:
You may use all pork with the mashed potatoes.

You may use 4 pounds of ground beef, 2 pounds of pork ground together. Instead of mashed potatoes, take 2 cups of barley and stir in hot water. Cook as you would a hot cereal until tender (about 30 minutes). Let cool before adding to meat.

These sausages are delicious and ready for company. *Note: My husband, our children, Grandmother Jones, who started it all, and I have fun early in December preparing these for the holidays.*
Mrs. Ernest A. Jones (Marian)
Oakland County (Bloomfield Hills)

. . . Place a bay leaf in flour, corn meal, etc. to keep weevils out.

CHICKEN TACOS

1 whole chicken
2 avocados, softened
1 large onion, chopped
¼ cup mayonnaise
Salt and pepper to taste
2 large tomatoes, thinly sliced
1 pound Cheddar cheese, grated
½ head lettuce, sliced
6 hot chili peppers, chopped (optional)
1 package corn tortillas (one per taco)
Cooking oil
Hot sauce (optional)

Bake chicken for 1 hour at 325 degrees. While chicken bakes, make guacamole sauce as follows: Mash avocados in bowl. Add 3 tablespoons chopped onions. Mix with mayonnaise and salt and pepper to taste. Next, put remainder of chopped onion, thinly sliced tomatoes, grated Cheddar cheese, sliced lettuce and chopped hot peppers in separate bowls. While chicken cools, fry corn tortilla shells in hot oil or deep fry for 10 seconds on each side (until slightly crisp). Slice chicken in small pieces. Arrange all ingredients as you wish on taco shell. *Note: You may wish to add hot sauce for some zip! Eat!*
Mrs. James Gilmore, Jr. (Diana)
Kalamazoo County (Kalamazoo)

International

EGG FOO YUNG

This recipe has quantities listed for service for 10.

Ingredients:	10
Onions, chopped in ¼-inch pieces	5 ounces
Celery, chopped in ¼-inch pieces	3 ounces
Mushrooms, stems and pieces	6 ounces
Bean Sprouts, well drained	6 ounces
Green Onion, chopped in ¼-inch pieces including green tops	¾ ounce
Salt	1½ teaspoons
Black pepper	¾ teaspoons
Accent	1½ teaspoons
Eggs	12
Shortening	To a depth of 1 inch in large frying pan
Egg Foo Yung Sauce	2 cups
Long grain rice	1 pound
Boiling water	1 quart
Salt	½ ounce

Combine onions, celery, mushrooms, bean sprouts and green onions. Beat eggs lightly and combine with salt, black pepper and Accent. Mix with vegetables. Combine in small amounts as close to cooking time as possible. Melt shortening to a depth of 1 inch in a large frying pan or roaster pan. Using a 4 ounce dipper, ladle egg mixture into hot fat. Turn when most of egg on top has set. Brown other side well, drain well. Arrange Egg Foo Yung in steamtable pans. Cover with Egg Foo Yung sauce and serve on a bed of rice. To prepare rice: Wash rice in cold water. Drain and drop into rapidly boiling water. Simmer approximately 20 minutes, or until tender. Strain. Wash off starch under cold then hot water until rice is reheated. Drain well.
Note: Cook Egg Foo Yung in small amounts as close to service as possible.

Ann E. Corwell
Oakland County (Pontiac)

... Remove vegetable stains from hands by rubbing with sliced raw potato.

CHOP SUEY CASSEROLE

1½ pounds ground beef
1 small onion, chopped
1 16-ounce can Chow Mein vegetables
1 can Campbell cream of mushroom soup
1 can Campbell cream of chicken soup
1 soup can water
½ cup raw rice
3 tablespoons soy sauce
1 3-ounce can Chow Mein noodles

Lightly brown ground beef and onions together in a frying pan. Using a 3-quart baking dish, combine the vegetables, soups, water, rice and soy sauce. Stir in the browned beef mixture. Cover the dish and bake at 350 degrees for 1 hour and 15 minutes, stirring once while baking to blend the rice. Uncover the dish and sprinkle with Chow Mein noodles. Return to oven and bake uncovered for another 10 minutes. *Note: This is a large recipe. It's fast and easy and you'll like it for pot lucks or large family meals. For smaller amounts, freeze half (unbaked and without noodles) for a busy day.*

Mrs. Vernon Brant (Joyce)
Newaygo County (Fremont)

CHOP SUEY

2½ pounds Chop Suey meat (pork, beef or veal), cubed
½ teaspoon salt
¼ teaspoon pepper
1 medium onion, chopped
1½ cups celery, diced
1 28-ounce can Chop Suey vegetables
1 16-ounce can bean sprouts
2 10-ounce cans cream of mushroom soup
1 8-ounce can mushrooms, drained
2 teaspoons soy sauce
2 cups water
2 cups rice
2 3-ounce cans Chow Mein noodles

Brown meat. Add salt, pepper, onion and celery, continue browning to transparent stage. Add Chop Suey vegetables, bean sprouts, soup, mushrooms, soy sauce and water. Cook at medium heat for 30 minutes. Reduce heat to simmer for additional 1½ hours, stirring occasionally, adding water if necessary. Prepare rice as directed on package. Serve Chop Suey over rice and chow mein noodles. Serves 8 to 10. *Note: Salt, pepper and soy sauce may be added depending on individual taste. Also Chop Suey may be thickened if desired.*

Brad Van Pelt
Shiawassee County (Owosso)

CHINESE EGG ROLLS

½ tablespoon soy sauce
1 teaspoon cornstarch
6 ounces lean pork, finely chopped
½ teaspoon salt
1 teaspoon cornstarch
4 ounces shrimp
5 tablespoons vegetable oil, divided
½ pound cabbage, finely chopped
8 ounces bean sprouts, thoroughly drained
½ cup cold water or chicken soup stock
1 teaspoon salt
1 tablespoon soy sauce
1 tablespoon cornstarch
1 tablespoon water
20 egg roll skins
1 tablespoon cold water
1 tablespoon flour

Combine ½ tablespoon soy sauce and 1 teaspoon cornstarch to form pork marinade. Sprinkle pork marinade over pork and stir. Combine ½ teaspoon salt and 1 teaspoon cornstarch to form shrimp marinade; sprinkle over shrimp and stir. Heat 2 tablespoons vegetable oil in wok, add pork and stir fry until white or all pink has disappeared (approximately 1 to 2 minutes). Remove and wipe wok clean. Add 1 tablespoon vegetable oil to wok, heat and stir fry shrimp 45 seconds. Remove and wipe wok clean. Add 2 tablespoons vegetable oil to wok, heat and stir fry scallions, cabbage and bean sprouts for 1½ minutes. Return pork and shrimp to wok, and sprinkle with mixture of water or chicken soup stock, 1 teaspoon salt and 1 tablespoon soy sauce. Heat all ingredients through. If necessary, add a thickening sauce made of 1 tablespoon cornstarch and 1 tablespoon water. Remove from wok, drain and cool. Place 1 heaping tablespoon of egg roll filling in each egg roll and roll tightly (See diagram below for rolling instructions.) Deep fry egg rolls in hot vegetable oil and keep turning until brown. Drain and serve hot. Serve with sweet-sour sauce and/or hot mustard sauce. Yield: 16 to 20 egg rolls. *Note: A number of steps are involved but well worth the time and effort.*

Dr. M. Jerome Edwards
Lenawee County (Adrian)

(Recipe continued on next page)

Rolling Instructions:
Place 1 round tablespoon filling in upper corner of wrapper. Fold corner over filling.

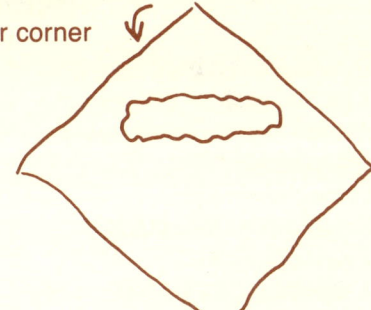

International

Roll skin to enclose filling, tucking in sides neatly.

On last corner of triangle, apply water and flour mixture with finger and seal.

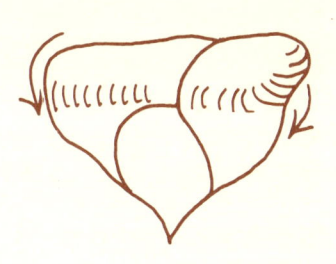

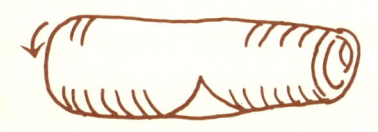

Continue rolling and place on tray sealed edge down. Deep fry in hot oil and keep turning until brown. Drain and serve hot.

International

PEPPER STEAK

1½ pound top beef round or sirloin steak, ¾ to 1-inch thick
¼ cup salad oil
1 cup water
1 medium onion, cut into ¼-inch slices
½ teaspoon garlic salt
¼ teaspoon ginger
2 medium green peppers, cut into ¾-inch strips
1 tablespoon cornstarch
2 to 3 teaspoons sugar (Optional)
2 tablespoons soy sauce
2 medium tomatoes, cut into ⅛-inch slices
Hot cooked rice

Trim fat from meat; cut meat into 2x¼-inch strips. Heat oil in large skillet and cook meat in oil, turning frequently, until brown (about 5 minutes.) Stir in water, onion, garlic salt and ginger. Heat to boiling. Reduce heat; cover and simmer 12 to 15 minutes for round steak, 5 to 8 minutes for sirloin. Add green pepper strips during last 5 minutes of simmering. Blend cornstarch, sugar and soy sauce together; stir into meat mixture. Cook, stirring constantly, until mixture thickens and boils. Boil and stir 1 minute. Cut each tomato into eighths; place on meat mixture. Cover; cook over low heat just until tomatoes are heated through (about 3 minutes). Serve over rice. Serves 4 to 5. *Note: Delicious served with rolls, a green salad and fresh fruit for dessert.*

Beverly Morin
Muskegon County (Muskegon)

RICE ORIENTAL

3 tablespoons salad oil
1 tablespoon onion, chopped
1½ cups beef, ham, pork, chicken, or turkey, cooked and diced
1⅓ cups Minute Rice
2 cups hot water
⅛ teaspoon pepper
1½ cups lettuce, shredded
2 tablespoons pimento, diced
2 tablespoons soy sauce

Heat oil in heavy skillet. Add onion and sauté until golden brown. Add meat, rice, pepper and hot water and mix just to moisten rice. Bring to boil over high heat, cover and remove from heat. Let stand 5 minutes. Just before serving, add lettuce, pimento and soy sauce. Toss lightly. *Note: Sprinkle with additional soy sauce when served.* Serves 4 to 5.

Margaret Wieda
Manistee County (Manistee)

SHRIMP MUSHROOM

1 pound shrimp, shelled and cleaned
1 egg white
1½ tablespoons cornstarch
½ teaspoon baking soda
½ cup vegetable oil
1 6-ounce can bamboo shoots, diced
1 6-ounce can water chestnuts, diced
2 stalks scallions, diced
1 6-ounce can button mushrooms
1½ teaspoons salt
1 teaspoon sugar
1 tablespoon sesame oil
1 tablespoon Sherry

Wash shrimp and towel dry. Marinate shrimp with egg white, cornstarch, and baking soda for 30 minutes. Heat ½ cup of vegetable oil in pan and stir fry shrimp. Take shrimp out when they start to turn white, but are not done. Use the remaining oil to stir fry bamboo shoots, water chestnuts, scallions, and mushrooms for 3 minutes. Add shrimp, salt, sugar, sesame oil and Sherry to mixture. Stir fry for 3 to 4 minutes. Serves 4.

Mrs. Ju-chien Wang
Macomb County (Warren)

. . . Pour a little vanilla on a piece of cotton and place in refrigerator to eliminate odors.

ZUCCHINI SAN LU RAE

4 tablespoons butter
1 small onion, finely chopped
½ teaspoon dried basil (or more if fresh)
4 cups zucchini, peeled, seeded and grated
Salt and pepper to taste

Melt butter in saucepan. Add onion and basil and sauté without browning, until onion is soft. Add zucchini and cook gently, stirring frequently, until zucchini is cooked but still just a little crisp. Season and serve hot. Serves 6. *Note: A wonderful way to use an old, fat zucchini.*

Rebecca Knack
Kent County (Grand Rapids)

International

LASAGNE

2 pounds ground steak
1 tablespoon olive oil
1 clove garlic, minced
3 tablespoons parsley flakes
2 teaspoons salt
2½ cups canned tomatoes
1 6-ounce can tomato paste
1 tablespoon dried basil
1 10-ounce package lasagne noodles

2 12-ounce cartons large curd cottage cheese
2 eggs, beaten
2 teaspoons salt
½ teaspoon pepper
1 cup Parmesan cheese, grated
1 pound Mozzarella cheese

Brown meat in hot oil in large skillet or heavy saucepan. Add garlic, 1 tablespoon parsley, 2 teaspoons salt, tomatoes, tomato paste and basil. Simmer, uncovered for 1 hour. Cook, drain and rinse noodles according to package directions. Combine cottage cheese, beaten eggs, salt, pepper, remaining 2 tablespoons parsley and Parmesan cheese. In a lightly greased baking dish, arrange alternate layers of noodles, cheese mixture and meat mixture, repeating until all is used. Cover top with Mozzarella cheese and bake in preheated 375 degree oven for 30 minutes. *Note: This may be put together ahead of time and frozen to be used at a later date.*

Leanor Buchanan
Branch County (Quincy)

ZABGLIONE

6 egg yolks
½ cup powdered sugar

½ cup Marsala wine
Pinch of cinnamon

Beat eggs with sugar until thick and lemon-colored. Put in top of double boiler over boiling water or in a heavy round bottomed bowl and set over boiling water. Beat constantly with an electric beater, adding wine little by little until mixture is beginning to hold its shape, but is still smooth. Remove from heat and pile mixture in glasses or cups. *Note: This recipe was given to me by the sister of Alfred Lunt.*

Dr. H. Marvin Pollard
Washtenaw County (Ann Arbor)

CHILIES RELLENOS

4 slices firm white bread
2 cups sharp Cheddar cheese, shredded
2 cups Monterey Jack cheese, shredded
2 4-ounce cans green chilies, minced
6 eggs
2 cups milk
2 teaspoons paprika
1 teaspoon salt
½ teaspoon ground oregano
½ teaspoon pepper
¼ teaspoon garlic powder
¼ teaspoon dry mustard

Remove crusts from bread and butter on one side. Place buttered side down in 7½x11½-inch baking dish. Sprinkle with Cheddar cheese, then with Monterey Jack. Spread chilies evenly over cheese. Beat eggs, add milk and all seasonings. Pour over cheese. Refrigerate 4 hours or overnight. Bake in 325 degree oven for 50 minutes. Let stand 10 minutes before serving. Serves 6. *Note: This is fantastic for brunch or supper—men love it!*

Mrs. F. W. Sassaman (Becky)
Eaton County (Charlotte)

CASSEROLE NAPOLI

1½ pounds ground beef
1 teaspoon salt
½ cup onion, chopped
1 29-ounce can tomato sauce
1 cup water
1 teaspoon oregano
8 ounces noodles or elbow macaroni
2 10-ounce packages frozen chopped spinach, thawed and drained
1 cup Ricotta or cottage cheese
½ cup sour cream
¼ cup Parmesan cheese, grated

Lightly brown meat in large skillet. Add salt and onion and cook another 5 minutes. Add tomato sauce, water and oregano. In another pan, cook noodles until done; drain, add to beef sauce. Combine sour cream and ricotta cheese. In a 9x13-inch pan, layer half of the noodle mixture; add the spinach in a layer and dollop half of the sour cream mixture. Top with remainder of noodles and rest of sour cream mixture. Sprinkle with Parmesan cheese. Bake at 375 degrees for 30 to 40 minutes. Serves 6 to 8. *Note: May be made ahead of time or frozen.*

Mrs. S. Charles Matloff (Lenore)
Washtenaw County (Chelsea)

International

YUGOSLAV KIFLE

2 cups flour, sifted
1 cake compressed yeast
1 stick margarine or butter
2 egg yolks

½ cup commercial sour cream
Powdered sugar
Margarine, melted

Put sifted flour into a large mixing bowl. Crumble in compressed yeast. Cut in margarine with pastry blender until mixture is crumbly. Add egg yolks and sour cream; mix well. Form into a ball. On lightly floured board, knead until smooth (5 to 10 minutes). Divide dough into 3 equal parts. Wrap in waxed paper. Chill in refrigerator at least 1 hour. On a board, sprinkle dough with powdered sugar, roll each of the three parts of the dough into an 8-inch circle. Cut each circle into 8 pie-shaped wedges. Fill wide end of each with 1 tablespoon of Walnut Filling (see below). Roll up from wide end to point. Place on greased baking sheets and brush with melted margarine. Bake at 375 degrees for about 25 minutes, or until golden brown. Dust with powdered sugar. Yield: 2 dozen cookies.

Walnut Filling:
1 cup walnuts, finely chopped
½ cup sugar

1 teaspoon vanilla
2 egg whites, stiffly beaten

Combine walnuts, sugar and vanilla. Fold in stiffly beaten egg whites. Makes enough filling for 2 dozen cookies.

Mrs. Ann May
Lake County (Chase)

DANISH KRINGLE

Dough:
4 cups flour
1 tablespoon sugar
1 teaspoon salt
3 packages dry yeast

1 cup margarine or butter
2 eggs
1 cup cold milk

Mix together flour, sugar, salt and yeast. Add shortening and mix thoroughly. Slightly beat eggs and milk. Add milk mixture all at once to the flour mixture. Cover and refrigerate overnight. To assemble, divide the dough into 6 parts. Roll each part into a rectangle on floured board. Add 2 tablespoons of filling in the center of dough and sprinkle with chopped nuts. Fold sides together overlapping the dough. Seal edges and ends. Place on ungreased cookie sheets (2 to a sheet). Let rise 1 hour only. Bake at 350 degrees for 15 minutes (should be golden brown). Frost with Icing. Yield: 6 pastries.

(Recipe continued on next page)

Filling:
1 cup granulated sugar
¾ cup butter or margarine
2 teaspoons cinnamon
1 cup walnut meats, chopped

Mix thoroughly all ingredients and fill pastry.

Icing:
2 cups powdered sugar
2 tablespoons milk
1 tablespoon margarine, melted
1 teaspoon vanilla

Blend all ingredients together thoroughly and ice baked Kringles.

Mrs. Louis Carter (Lorene)
Presque Isle County (Rogers City)

FINNISH SWEET ROLLS

4 cups flour
1 teaspoon salt
¼ cup sugar
1 cup margarine, softened
1 package dry yeast dissolved in ¼ cup very warm water
3 egg yolks, beaten
1 cup milk, scalded and cooled
¼ cup sugar
¾ teaspoon cinnamon

Put flour, salt and sugar into large bowl. Cut in margarine until mixture looks like corn meal. Add the yeast which has been dissolved in water along with egg yolks and cooked milk. Beat well. Chill in refrigerator overnight. Grease well about 24 muffin cups. Roll ½ of chilled dough into a 12x18-inch rectangle. Brush with melted margarine or butter generously. Then sprinkle with mixture of ¼ cup sugar and ¾ teaspoon cinnamon. Beginning at wide end as for jellyroll, cut into 1 inch slices and place in muffin cups. Roll and cut other ½ of dough the same way. Cover and let rise in warm place for 1 hour. Bake at 350 degrees for 20 to 25 minutes until golden brown. Remove from pans while hot and frost with creamy glaze.

Glaze:
½ cup powdered sugar
2 tablespoons butter
1½ teaspoons vanilla
1 to 2 teaspoons hot water

Mix all ingredients together to make medium thick glaze. Frost sweet rolls.

Mrs. William Kitti (Ellen)
Kalkaska County (Kalkaska)

International

PASCHALINE PSOMI
(Greek Easter Bread)

¼ cup honey
½ teaspoon cardamon, ground
¾ teaspoon salt
3 tablespoons Fleischmann's margarine
½ teaspoon orange rind

1 package yeast dissolved in ¼ cup milk (105°)
¼ cup orange juice
3 eggs
1½ cups flour
3 raw eggs dyed red

Combine honey, cardamon, salt, margarine and orange rind in Kitchen-Aid bowl and mix with batter beater on first speed for a few seconds. Add yeast mixture and orange juice. Using batter beater on fourth speed for 2 minutes, develop gluten in flour. Add 3 eggs, one at a time and mix into batter for 1 minute on fourth speed. Switch to dough hook and add 1½ cups flour gradually. More flour may be necessary, depending on the weather (humidity). Dough should be tacky. Set dough in greased ceramic bowl and allow to rise for about 2 hours until double in bulk. Knead dough, setting aside a small portion of dough for braided decoration. Have ready the 3 raw eggs dyed red. Shape dough and place in greased 10-inch pan. Make 3 braids from reserved dough (symbolic of wreath on Christ's head when He was crucified). Place wreaths on top of bread with a red egg in the middle of each braid. Allow to rise about 1½ hours. Bake at 375 degrees for 20 minutes. Brush gently with glaze and bake another 10 to 15 minutes.

Glaze:
1 egg white
1 tablespoon water

1 teaspoon sugar

Mix glaze ingredients in a cup and gently brush on top of bread around the eggs, trying not to touch them.

Toula Patsalis, Owner
Kitchen Glamor
Wayne County (Detroit)

. . . Wrap a piece of adhesive tape around your first finger when peeling large quantities of fruits or vegetables. Tape will prevent you from cutting fingers.

This section was
made possible by a gift from
Chelsea Milling Company.

Desserts

Desserts

The first six recipes in this section were provided by Chelsea Milling Company.

FUDGE CREAM BARS

1 cup Jiffy Baking Mix
1 package Jiffy Fudge Frosting Mix
⅓ cup butter
½ cup nuts, chopped

1 8-ounce package cream cheese
Fudge Frosting Mix
1 teaspoon vanilla
1 egg

Preheat oven to 350 degrees. In a large bowl, combine Jiffy Baking Mix, 1¼ cups Fudge Frosting Mix and butter. Blend at low speed until well mixed and crumbly. Stir in nuts. In small bowl, beat cream cheese until smooth. Add remaining Fudge Frosting Mix (about ⅔ cup), vanilla and egg. Blend thoroughly. Press firmly about 2 cups of Baking Mix mixture into an ungreased 8-inch square pan. Spread with cream cheese filling. Sprinkle remaining 1 cup Baking Mix mixture on top. Bake about 35 minutes, or until toothpick inserted in center comes out clean. Chill and cut in squares. Store in refrigerator. Yield: Sixteen 2-inch squares.

IMPOSSIBLE PIE

4 eggs
1 cup sugar
½ cup Jiffy Baking Mix
½ stick butter

2 cups milk
1 teasoon vanilla
½ teaspoon nutmeg

Heat oven to 350 degrees. Grease a 9-inch pie pan. Mix all ingredients together in blender or mixer (about 5 minutes at medium speed). Pour into pie pan and bake about 45 minutes.

FRUIT MAGIC

1 1 pound 5-ounce can cherry pie filling
1 package Jiffy White Cake Mix

¼ cup margarine, softened
½ cup nuts, chopped (Optional)

Preheat oven to 350 degrees. Spread pie filling in 8x8-inch square pan. Combine cake mix and nuts in bowl. Add softened margarine and mix until crumbly. Sprinkle over top of pie filling. Bake 45 to 50 minutes until golden brown. Serves 6.

HAWAIIAN DESSERT

1 package Jiffy Yellow Cake Mix
1 egg
½ cup water

Prepare cake as directed on package. Bake at 350 degrees in greased 9x13-inch pan for 20 minutes.

Frosting:
1 package instant pudding mix
1 cup milk
4 ounces cream cheese
1 large can crushed pineapple, drained
1 package Dream Whip

Mix pudding mix, milk and cream cheese together. Spread over cooled cake. Spread drained pineapple over pudding mixture. Prepare Dream Whip as directed on package and spread over pineapple mixture. Sprinkle with coconut if desired.

BASIC CRÊPES

2 cups Jiffy Baking Mix
1¼ cups water
2 eggs

Place all ingredients in mixing bowl and beat well. Pour ¼ cup batter on lightly greased 8-inch skillet. Rotate pan until batter covers bottom. Bake until bubbles appear. Gently loosen edge and turn and bake on other side. Place a scoop of your favorite ice cream on each crêpe. Fold and cover with hot dessert sauce of your choice, or fruit preserve. Yield: Twelve 8-inch crêpes.

Blintzes:
1 3-ounce package cream cheese
⅔ cup cottage cheese
¼ cup sugar
1 teaspoon vanilla
2 tablespoons butter, melted
Confectioners' sugar
1 cup strawberry preserves

Blend cheeses with sugar and vanilla. Fill each crêpe with 1 rounded tablespoon. Fold. Brush with melted butter and serve sprinkled with sugar and preserves.

GELATIN MAGIC

1 package Jiffy White Cake Mix
2 eggs
5 tablespoons instant vanilla pudding mix
¼ cup butter or margarine, softened
½ cup water
1 3-ounce package favorite flavor gelatin

Preheat oven to 350 degrees and generously grease and dust with flour an 8x8-inch square pan. Combine cake mix, eggs, pudding mix, butter and water and beat 3 minutes at medium speed. Bake 35 to 40 minutes or until a toothpick inserted in center comes out clean. Prepare gelatin with 1 cup boiling water. Set aside. Remove cake from oven. Prick with fork at ½-inch intervals. Pour gelatin over cake while hot and refrigerate until set. Cover with your favorite topping if desired.

CHOCOLATE SHEATH CAKE AND FROSTING

1 stick margarine
3½ tablespoons cocoa
½ cup Crisco
1 cup water
2 cups flour
2 cups sugar
2 eggs
1 teaspoon vanilla
½ cup buttermilk
1 teaspoon baking soda

Melt margarine, cocoa, Crisco and water and bring them to a boil. Combine flour and sugar then stir in the cocoa mixture thoroughly. Add the unbeaten eggs and vanilla, stirring well. Mix the baking soda with the buttermilk and pour into the batter and mix again. Spread this batter into a greased 18x12x1-inch pan. Bake at 400 degrees for 15 to 20 minutes. Frost the cake hot from the oven. Serves 36.

Frosting:
⅓ cup milk
1 stick margarine
3½ tablespoons cocoa
1 pound powdered sugar
1 teaspoon vanilla
2 cups nuts

Five minutes before the cake is done begin preparing the frosting. In a saucepan, melt the milk, margarine and cocoa and bring to a boil. Stir in powdered sugar, vanilla and nuts. Pour the hot frosting over the hot cake.

Rose Marie Thering
Clinton County (Elsie)

Janice Roestel
Huron County (Pigeon)

CHOCOLATE PUDDING CAKE

¾ cup sugar
3 tablespoons butter
2 tablespoons cocoa
1 cup flour
2 teaspoons baking powder
⅛ teaspoon salt
½ cup milk
½ cup nuts, chopped (Optional)
1 teaspoon vanilla

Combine all of the above ingredients in an ungreased 8x8-inch pan and mix well with a spoon. Top with pudding mixture and bake at 350 degrees for 30 minutes. *Note: Delicious served warm with ice cream!*

Pudding Mixture:
¾ cup brown sugar
¾ cup white sugar
3 tablespoons cocoa
1¾ cup boiling water

Combine ingredients and stir. Pour over cake mixture.

Beverly Scott and Sherry Dean
Ogemaw County (West Branch)

CHOCOLATE CAKE

½ cup cocoa
2 cups flour
2 cups sugar
1 teaspoon salt
½ cup shortening
2 eggs
½ cup sour milk
1½ teaspoons soda
1 teaspoon vanilla
1 cup boiling water

Place cocoa, flour, sugar and salt in mixing bowl and mix thoroughly. Add shortening, eggs and vanilla. Dissolve soda in sour milk and add to mixture. Mix thoroughly. Add boiling water and mix thoroughly. Pour into greased and floured 9x13-inch pan. Bake at 350 degrees for about 35 minutes. Or use two greased and floured 9-inch pans and bake for about 25 minutes. *Note: Do not overbake. Cake is done when a toothpick inserted into cake comes out clean.*

Mrs. Norbert Hanson
Menominee County (Wallace)

Desserts

WACKY CAKE

1½ cups flour
1 cup sugar
3 tablespoons cocoa
1 teaspoon soda
½ teaspoon salt

6 tablespoons salad oil
1 tablespoon vinegar
1 teaspoon vanilla
1 cup cold water

Sift flour, sugar, cocoa, soda and salt into an ungreased 8x8x2-inch pan. Pour oil, vinegar, vanilla and water over dry mixture. Stir well with fork. Bake at 350 degrees for 25 minutes.

Thelma Endicott
Branch County (Coldwater)

LEMON CHEESE CAKE

Graham Cracker Crust:
1¼ cups graham cracker crumbs

3 tablespoons sugar
⅓ cup butter, melted

Combine graham cracker crumbs and sugar in medium-size bowl. Stir in melted butter until thoroughly blended. Pack mixture firmly into one 9-inch pie pan and press firmly to bottom and sides of pan, bringing crumbs up to rim. Chill for 1 hour before filling or bake at 350 degrees for 8 minutes. Cook, chill and fill. If desired, pie pan may be buttered.

Lemon Cheese Cake Filling:
4 3-ounce packages cream cheese
1 cup fresh lemon juice

2 eggs, beaten
1 cup sugar

Blend cream cheese and lemon juice. Add eggs and beat until smooth. Add sugar and blend thoroughly. Pour into Graham Cracker Crust. Bake in 350 degree oven for 15 to 20 minutes. Cool 5 minutes.

Topping:
1 cup sour cream

1 tablespoon lemon rind, grated

Mix lemon rind and sour cream. Spread topping on cheese cake. After completely cool (approximately 3 hours), bake at 350 degrees for 10 more minutes. Chill and serve.

Prosser M. Watts, Jr.
Lenawee County (Adrian)

14 KARAT CAKE

2 teaspoons cinnamon
2 cups flour
2 teaspoons baking powder
1½ teaspoons soda
1½ teaspoons salt
2 cups sugar
1½ cups salad oil
4 eggs
½ cup nutmeats
1 8-ounce can crushed pineapple, drained
2½ ounces shredded coconut
2 cups shredded carrots

Combine cinnamon, flour, baking powder, soda, salt, sugar, salad oil and eggs. Mix well. Then add nuts, pineapple, coconut and carrots. Bake at 350 degrees for 40 to 50 minutes. Yield: One 3 layer cake.

Cream Cheese Frosting:
1 stick butter
1 pound powdered sugar
8 ounces Philadelphia cream cheese
1 teaspoon vanilla
Milk to thin

Combine frosting ingredients. *Yummy!*

Mrs. Earl Detweiler (Vera)
Oscoda County (Mio)

DREAM CAKE

1 cup all-purpose flour
½ cup margarine or butter
¼ cup brown sugar
1½ cups brown sugar
2 eggs
¾ cup walnuts, chopped
1 cup coconut
2 tablespoons flour
½ teaspoon baking powder
¼ teaspoon salt
½ teaspoon vanilla

Mix flour, butter and ¼ cup brown sugar as for pie crust. Spread evenly in a 9x9-inch pan. Bake in 300 degree oven until slightly puffed and golden brown. If you wish, strawberry or raspberry jam may be spread over this after you remove from oven. Mix 1½ cups brown sugar, eggs, walnuts, coconut, flour, baking powder, salt and vanilla and spread on top of pastry. Bake at 300 degrees for 25 minutes. Remove from oven, cool, and cut into small squares. *Rich, but delicious!*

Mrs. Edward Scully (Jean)
Monroe County (Monroe)

Desserts

ECLAIR CAKE

1 box Honey Graham crackers
2 packages French Vanilla instant pudding
1 9-ounce carton Cool Whip

Butter bottom of 9x13-inch pan and line with graham cracker squares. Prepare pudding according to package directions using ¼ less milk. Cool. Blend in Cool Whip. Pour ½ pudding mixture over graham crackers. Add another layer of crackers then another layer of pudding. Top with graham crackers. Frost and chill for 2 days before serving. Cut into squares to serve.

Frosting:
2 packages Ready Blend chocolate
2 tablespoons white corn syrup
1 teaspoon vanilla
1 tablespoon milk
2 tablespoons mayonnaise, melted
1½ cups powdered sugar

Mix all ingredients together and frost top layer of graham crackers.

Mrs. Carl Wolgamott
Lake County (Baldwin)

TILLIE'S FRENCH PASTRY CAKE

7 large eggs, separated
½ teaspoon cream of tartar
2 cups flour
3 teaspoons baking powder
1 teaspoon salt
1½ cups sugar
½ cup Wesson or Mazola salad oil
¾ cup cold water
1 teaspoon vanilla extract
1 teaspoon lemon extract

Separate eggs, putting whites in large bowl. Add cream of tartar and beat until very stiff. In another bowl, sift flour, baking powder, salt and sugar. Add egg yolks, oil, water, flavorings. Beat with mixer until well blended. Fold flour and egg yolk mixture into beaten egg whites with rubber scraper until well blended. Pour in two oblong 9x13-inch pans or three 8 or 9-inch pans. *Do not grease pans.* Foil pans may be used. Turn pans upside down on rack or containers so air can reach cake. Recipe will make 3 dozen cup cakes. Fill paper cups to ¾ full and take out immediately from pans after baking. Set on counter to cool. Bake at 350 degrees for 45 to 55 minutes. Tme depends on size of pans. Cake is done when golden brown. *Note: Ideal cake for French pastries and petit-fours.*

Tillie Van Oosterhout
St. Joseph County (Three Rivers)

HILLBILLY CAKE

2 eggs
1 can No. 2 pineapple
2 cups flour
1 teaspoon soda

⅛ teaspoon salt
1½ cups sugar
1 cup coconut

Mix eggs and pineapple and set aside. Combine flour, soda, salt and sugar and mix together. Combine with eggs and pineapple. Pour into 9x13x2-inch pan and top with coconut. Bake at 350 degrees for 45 minutes.

Topping:
1 cup milk
1 cup sugar

1 stick butter

Combine milk, sugar and butter and boil for 3 minutes. Punch holes in top of cake with fork and spoon frosting over top.

Verda Hayward
Lapeer County (Lapeer)

GRANDMA CAKE

1½ cups sugar
2 cups flour
1 teaspoon baking soda
1 teaspoon salt
1 20-ounce can crushed pineapple, not drained

2 eggs
¾ cup brown sugar
½ cup walnuts, chopped

Mix together sugar, flour, baking soda and salt. Add pineapple and eggs. Beat and pour into a 9x13-inch greased pan. Sprinkle with brown sugar and walnuts before baking. Bake at 350 degrees for 40 to 45 minutes. Frost hot cake.

Frosting:
1 stick margarine, melted
½ cup sugar

1 teaspoon vanilla
1 large can Pet milk

Combine frosting ingredients in saucepan. Bring to a full boil. Pour slowly over hot cake. Serve warm or cold.

Peggy Le Blanc
Cheboygan County (Cheboygan)

JUICY PINEAPPLE CAKE WITH BUTTER SAUCE

2 cups sugar
2 cups flour
1 teaspoon baking soda
Dash of salt

2 eggs
1 20-ounce can crushed
  pineapple, undrained

Place all ingredients in mixer bowl and blend at low speed, scraping bowl. Beat at medium speed for 2 minutes. Pour into greased 9x13-inch pan and bake at 350 degrees for 30 to 40 minutes. Remove from oven and immediately poke holes in warm cake with a toothpick or meat fork. Then pour Butter Sauce over cake, slowly allowing it to soak into cake. Use a rubber spatula to scrape the excess sauce from the edges to the middle of the cake until all sauce is absorbed.

Butter Sauce:
1 stick margarine
1 cup sugar

1 cup evaporated milk
1 teaspoon vanilla

Make sauce while cake bakes. Melt margarine in a saucepan. Add the sugar, evaporated milk and vanilla, and cook over low heat until the sugar is dissolved. Keep warm until the cake is baked, then immediately pour over cake as directed above.

Mrs. Robert Rander (Andrea)
Ottawa County (Conklin)

POPPY SEED CAKE

1½ cups vegetable oil
2 cups granulated sugar
4 eggs
1 12-ounce can Solo poppy
  seed

1 13-ounce can evaporated milk
3 cups flour
1 teaspoon baking soda
1 teaspoon baking powder
1 teaspoon salt

Combine all ingredients in a large bowl and mix for 3 to 5 minutes on high speed with an electric mixer. Pour into ungreased tube pan and bake at 350 degrees for 1 hour and 15 minutes. When cool, dust with powdered sugar or top with confectioners' sugar icing. Serves 24.

Mrs. Donald Longfield (Sylvia)
Kalkaska County (Kalkaska)

JIFFY PINEAPPLE DREAM CAKE

1 9-ounce package Jiffy white cake mix
1 egg
½ cup water

Prepare Jiffy white cake mix according to package instructions, using the egg and water. Place in a greased 9x13-inch cake pan. Bake at 350 degrees for 10 minutes, or until done. Cool cake and frost. *Note: This will make a very thin layer as the cake mix is for a single layer cake, so be sure to bake only 10 minutes.*

Frosting:
1 8-ounce package cream cheese, softened
2 cups cold milk
1 3½-ounce package vanilla instant pudding
1 large can crushed pineapple, drained
1 large carton prepared whipped topping

Beat softened cream cheese with milk until well blended and creamy. Add instant pudding mix to cream cheese and milk mixture. Pour this on cooled cake and spread evenly. Drain the crushed pineapple and place evenly on the pudding layer. Cover all with prepared whipped topping. Keep in refrigerator until serving. Serve in squares.

Mrs. Roscoe Stuber (Barbara)
Livingston County (Howell)

POTATO CAKE

1 cup Crisco
2 cups sugar
4 eggs, separated
1 teaspoon each nutmeg, cinnamon, and cloves
2 teaspoons cocoa
1 cup potatoes, cooked and mashed
1 cup pecans, chopped
2 cups flour, sifted
2 teaspoons baking powder
½ cup milk

Cream shortening and sugar; add egg yolks, spices, cocoa, potatoes and pecans. Mix flour and baking powder. Add to creamed mixture alternately with milk. Fold in stiffly beaten egg whites. Bake at 350 degrees in tube pan for 1 hour. Serves 20.

Mrs. John Masar (Helen I.)
Gratiot County (Breckenridge)

Desserts

COOKIE SHEET CAKE

2 cups flour
2 cups sugar
1 teaspoon soda
½ teaspoon salt
1 teaspoon cinnamon
1 stick margarine
½ cup Crisco

4 tablespoons cocoa or 1 square chocolate
1 cup water
½ cup buttermilk or ½ cup milk with 1½ teaspoons vinegar
1 teaspoon vanilla
2 eggs, beaten

Mix flour, sugar, soda, salt and cinnamon together. In saucepan, melt margarine, Crisco, cocoa or chocolate and water. Pour mixture over dry ingredients. Add buttermilk or milk and vinegar mixture, vanilla and eggs and mix. Pour into greased cookie sheet. Bake at 350 degrees for 20 minutes. Let cool for 15 minutes and frost.

Frosting:
1 stick margarine
1 square chocolate or 5 tablespoons cocoa
4 or 5 tablespoons milk

1 1-pound box XX sugar
1 teaspoon vanilla
½ cup milk

Melt margarine, chocolate and milk together. Add XX sugar, vanilla and nuts. Frost cooled cake.

Mrs. Bryan McLay (Peggy)
Muskegon County (Norton Shores)

. . . Do not grease the sides of a cake pan.

SPICE BUNDT CAKE

2 cups self-rising-flour, sifted
1 cup Wesson oil
1 teaspoon cloves
1 8-ounce jar applesauce or 2 baby food jars of any fruit

2 cups sugar
4 eggs
1 teaspoon cinnamon
1 cup nuts, chopped (Optional)

Place all ingredients except nuts in mixer. Beat until creamy and thick. Add nuts. Pour batter into greased bundt pan. Bake at 350 degrees for 50 to 60 minutes. Cool. *Note: Good served plain or with whipped topping.*

Mrs. John Quinn (Arlene)
Lapeer County (Lapeer)

CARROT CAKE

3 eggs
2 cups sugar
1 cup vegetable oil
1 teaspoon salt
1 teaspoon baking soda
1 teaspoon cinnamon

2 cups flour
2 cups carrots, grated
1 cup nuts, chopped
1 cup crushed pineapple, drained
1 teaspoon vanilla

Combine eggs, sugar, and oil; mix until smooth. Add salt, soda, cinnamon and flour one at a time. Add carrots, nuts, pineapple and vanilla. Bake at 350 degrees for 40 to 60 minutes or until done. *Note: No other liquid is needed for this recipe.*

Icing:
1 cup milk
2 tablespoons cornstarch
½ cup margarine, softened

½ cup Crisco
¼ cup sugar
Vanilla

In small saucepan combine milk and cornstarch. Stir over medium heat until thick. Remove from heat and let cool. Add margarine, Crisco, sugar and vanilla. Beat until fluffy.

Mrs. Ardith P. Conroy
Cheboygan County (Wolverine)

PINEAPPLE CAKE

2 eggs, beaten
1½ cups sugar
1 No. 2 can crushed
   pineapple, undrained
1 teaspoon vanilla

2½ cups flour
2 teaspoons soda
½ teaspoon salt
½ cup nuts, chopped (Optional)

Add sugar to eggs and beat well. Add pineapple and vanilla. Sift flour, soda and salt and add to pineapple mixture. Fold in nuts. Bake in 13x9-inch pan for 30 minutes in 350 degree oven. Cool and spread with topping.

Topping:
1 stick margarine, softened
1 8-ounce package cream
   cheese

1¾ cups powdered sugar
1 teaspoon vanilla
½ cup nuts, chopped

Mix margarine and cream cheese. Add powdered sugar, vanilla and nuts and spread on cake. *Note: Cake keeps well in refrigerator for week or more.*

Mrs. Wayne R. Stark
Oscoda County (Mio)

Desserts

GRANNY CAKE

2 cups flour
1½ cups sugar
1 teaspoon soda
1 teaspoon salt
2 eggs

1 18-ounce can crushed
    pineapple, undrained
½ cup brown sugar
½ cup nutmeats

Mix well flour, sugar, soda and salt. Add 2 eggs and pineapple. Pour into a greased 9x13-inch pan. Top with mixture of brown sugar and nut meats. Bake at 350 degrees for 35 to 40 minutes. After baking cake for 30 minutes, prepare your topping.

Topping:
½ stick margarine
½ cup sugar

1 cup Pet milk
1 teaspoon vanilla

In heavy saucepan combine all ingredients. Stir until the sugar dissolves and boil for 1 minute. Cook cake about 1 minute. Pour topping over cake and let set.

Mrs. Carolyn Coulson
Gratiot County (Breckenridge)

. . . To keep icing from running off a cake, dust a little flour on the cake's surface.

TOMATO SOUP CAKE

½ cup butter or oleo, softened
1 cup sugar
1 teaspoon soda
1 teaspoon salt
1 teaspoon nutmeg
1 teaspoon cinnamon

1 teaspoon cloves
2 cups flour
1 cup tomato soup
½ cup walnut meats, chopped
1 cup dates, chopped

Cream butter and add sugar. Sift soda, salt, nutmeg, cinnamon, cloves and flour and add to creamed mixture alternately with tomato soup. Fold in nuts and dates. Bake in loaf pan at 350 degrees for 1 hour. You may use a 7x15-inch cake pan and bake for 35 minutes. Serves 20.

Marian E. Bussa
Antrim County (Rapid City)

TEXAS SHEET CAKE

2 cups flour
2 cups sugar
2 eggs
1 teaspoon salt
½ cup sour cream
1 teaspoon soda
1 cup water
2 sticks margarine
4 tablespoons cocoa

Combine flour, sugar, eggs, salt, sour cream and soda. Mix well. Heat water, margarine, and cocoa in saucepan and bring to boiling point. Add cocoa mixture to flour and beat until smooth (can use mixer). Pour into greased and floured jellyroll pan or cookie sheet. Bake at 350 degrees for 20 minutes. While warm ice with Topping. *Note: Batter is thin but is delicious. Will keep moist for several days.*

Topping:
1 stick margarine
6 tablespoons milk
4 tablespoons cocoa
1 pound powdered sugar
1 cup nuts, chopped

Combine margarine, milk and cocoa in saucepan. Bring to boil. Add to powdered sugar and stir until smooth. Add nuts. Ice warm cake.

Ruby Veliquette
Antrim County (Elk Rapids)

PUMPKIN PIE CAKE

1 20¼-ounce box white cake mix, divided
1 egg
⅓ cup margarine, melted
2 cups pumpkin
2 eggs
½ cup brown sugar
2½ teaspoons pumpkin pie spice
¼ cup white sugar
1 teaspoon cinnamon
3 tablespoons margarine, softened not melted

Reserve 1 cup of white cake mix. Mix the remaining cake mix in bowl with 1 egg and ⅓ cup melted margarine. Place evenly in a greased 9x13-inch pan. Then in bowl mix pumpkin, 2 eggs, brown sugar and pumpkin pie spice together and pour over first layer. Put the reserved white cake mix in a small bowl and combine with white sugar, cinnamon and softened margarine. Thoroughly mix with fingers and sprinkle over pumpkin layer. Bake at 350 degrees for 45 to 50 minutes. Serves 12 to 15.

Mrs. Clarence Laur (Terrie)
Bay County (Pinconning)

Desserts

RED VELVET CAKE

1½ cups sugar
½ cup Crisco
2 eggs
2 ounces red food coloring
2 tablespoons cocoa
2½ cups flour

1 teaspoon salt
1 cup buttermilk
1 teaspoon vanilla
1 tablespoon vinegar
1 teaspoon soda

Cream sugar and Crisco until fluffy. Add eggs one at a time and beat well after each addition. Add food coloring and cocoa; beat well. Add flour and salt alternately with buttermilk. Beat well. Add vanilla and mix well. Remove beaters from batter. Mix together vinegar and soda in small glass and immediately add to batter. Mix well with a spoon. Pour in 2 greased and floured layer pans that have been lined with waxed paper. Bake at 330 degrees for 30 to 45 minutes. Cool cake and cut layers in half to frost.

Frosting:
1⅓ cups milk
⅓ cup flour
2 cups powdered sugar

½ pound Fleischman's margarine
½ teaspoon vanilla
½ teaspoon almond flavoring

Use enough milk to make flour into thickening and put the rest of milk in saucepan to boil. Add thickening to milk and stir until thick. Set aside to cool. Mixture must be thoroughly cooled. Beat sugar and margarine until light and thick. Add paste and beat well, until consistency of whipped cream. Add flavorings. Frosting will look a little curdily. *Note: If you don't wish to buy a quart of buttermilk and have recipes such as this cake calling for a small amount, make your own. Combine 1 tablespoon lemon juice with enough milk to make 1 cup. Let stand 5 minutes.*

Mrs. Ann Pattee
Osceola County (Evart)

BUTTER CREAM FROSTING

1 cup granulated sugar
¾ cup Carnation or Pet milk
1 egg white

¾ cup Crisco or Spry shortening
1 teaspoon vanilla

Add all ingredients in a small mixing bowl. Beat for 15 minutes at a high speed until thick. *Note: For best results, make only one batch at a time.*

Representative Francis Spaniola
Shiawassee County (Corunna)

FOOLPROOF PIE CRUST

1 tablespoon vinegar
1 cup milk
1¾ cups lard

4 cups flour
¼ teaspoon salt
1 egg

Add vinegar to milk and set aside. Cut lard into flour and salt until size of small peas. Add egg and milk to flour mixture and mix well. Chill before using. *Note: Makes enough for 2 double crust pies and freezes well.*

Mrs. Gerry Walling
Otsego County (Gaylord)

BASIC CREAM PIE FILLING AND VARIATIONS

2 cups milk, scalded
⅓ cup flour
⅔ cup sugar
¼ teaspoon salt
3 egg yolks, beaten
2 tablespoons butter

½ teaspoon vanilla
3 egg whites
6 tablespoons sugar
¼ teaspoon cream of tartar
½ teaspoon salt
½ teaspoon vanilla

Scald milk and add flour, sugar and salt. Stir and cook until thick. Add beaten egg yolks, butter and vanilla and cook 1 minute longer stirring. (For variations, either add or substitute at proper time.) Pour filling in one baked 9-inch pie crust. To make meringue, beat egg whites until fluffy. Add sugar 1 tablespoon at a time along with the cream of tartar, salt, and vanilla. Beat until egg whites hold their shape. Pile meringue on filling and bake in 350 degree oven for 12 minutes.

Variations:
Pineapple Cream—Add ½ cup drained pineapple
Date Cream—Add 1 cup chopped dates
Coconut Cream—Add 1 cup coconut and use ¼ cup coconut on meringue
Caramel—Caramelize ¼ cup sugar
Butterscotch—Add 3 tablespoons butter and use 1 cup dark brown sugar instead of white sugar
Banana Cream—Add sliced bananas

Mrs. Arletta Hamilton
Newaygo County (Fremont)

Desserts

ANGEL CHEESECAKE PIE

1 10-inch graham cracker crust
½ cup sugar
1 envelope Knox gelatin
¼ teaspoon salt
1 egg, separated
½ cup milk
1 12-ounce package cream cheese
2 tablespoons lemon juice
2 tablespoons sugar
1 cup whipping cream

Combine ½ cup sugar, gelatin, salt, egg yolk and milk in saucepan. Cook, stirring constantly, until mixture boils. Remove from heat and add cream cheese and lemon juice to mixture. Beat well and chill in refrigerator until very thick, but not set. Beat egg white until stiff, adding 2 tablespoons sugar. Fold into cheese mixture. Beat whipping cream and fold in. Pour into graham cracker crusts and top with graham cracker crumbs. Allow to set in refrigerator for 2 hours. Serves 8.

Charlene Hutchinson
Cheboygan County (Topinabee)

FRENCH SILK PIE

Crust:
2 tablespoons butter, softened   1½ cups shredded coconut

Spread softened butter on pie pan and press in shredded coconut. Cook at 350 degrees for 12 to 15 minutes.

Filling:
½ cup butter
¾ cup sugar
1 square baking chocolate, melted
1 teaspoon vanilla
2 eggs
1 cup nuts

Cream butter and sugar together. Add melted baking chocolate and vanilla, blending well. Add 2 eggs, one at a time beating 5 minutes after each addition. Fold in nuts. Turn into shell and chill for 2 hours. *Note: For a festive touch, serve with whipped cream garnished with nuts and chocolate swirls.*

Mrs. Peter Henricksen (Ann)
Marquette County (Marquette)

CHOCOLATE PIE

1 pie crust, baked and hot
2 cups canned milk
2 egg yolks
¾ cup sugar
3 tablespoons flour

½ teaspoon salt
1 teaspoon vanilla
2 squares unsweetened chocolate
(cut in small pieces)

Scald 1½ cups milk in double boiler. Meanwhile, mix remaining ½ cup milk with egg yolks, sugar, flour, salt, vanilla and chocolate pieces. Add scalded milk gradually to chocolate mixture, then return to double boiler and cook, stirring constantly until mixture becomes very thick. Pour into a hot pie crust (pie crust won't be soggy when both mixtures are hot) and cool to room temperature. Chill for several hours and serve with whipped cream topping spread over entire pie. Serves 8.

Whipped Cream Topping:
1 teaspoon vanilla
¼ cup superfine sugar

½ pint whipping cream

Combine ingredients and beat well. Serve over chilled pie.

Mrs. George Spaulding (Dorie)
Oakland County (Bloomfield Hills)

COCONUT OR BANANA CREAM PIE

1 10-inch pie shell, baked
3 cups hot milk
3 tablespoons cornstarch
¾ cup sugar

¾ teaspoon salt
3 eggs, separated
3 teaspoons vanilla
½ cup coconut or 2 bananas

Scald milk in double boiler. Mix cornstarch, sugar and salt. Add slowly to hot milk. Cook 20 minutes over hot water. Beat egg yolks and add slowly to milk mixture stirring rapidly. Cool and add vanilla. Slice bananas into pie shell and fill with cream. Beat egg whites with a little bit of sugar until stiff. Spread meringue on top of pie and brown in oven. (For coconut pie, add coconut to milk mixture and cover with meringue. Sprinkle coconut on top of meringue.)

Lorraine Knight
Isabella County (Mt. Pleasant)

Desserts

E-Z COCONUT PIE

2 cups milk
½ cup Jiffy baking mix
¾ cup sugar
4 eggs

¼ cup margarine
1½ teaspoons vanilla
1 cup flake coconut

Combine milk, baking mix, sugar, eggs, margarine and vanilla in electric blender. Cover and blend on low speed for 3 minutes. Pour into greased 9-inch pie pan. Let stand 5 minutes, then sprinkle with coconut. Bake at 350 degrees for 40 minutes. Serve warm or cold. Serves 6.

Sally Arnett
Livingston County (Howell)

AMAZING COCONUT PIE

2 cups milk
¾ cup sugar
½ cup dry biscuit mix
4 eggs

¼ cup butter, cut into bits
1½ teaspoons vanilla
1 cup flaked coconut

Place milk, sugar, biscuit mix, eggs, butter and vanilla in electric blender container. Cover and blend on low for 3 minutes. Pour into greased 9-inch pie pan. Let stand about 5 minutes; sprinkle with coconut. Bake at 350 degrees for 40 minutes. Serve warm or cool.

Mrs. Elfriede Kadwell
Lake County (Chase)

PEANUT BUTTER PIE

1 8 or 9-inch graham cracker pie shell
1 3-ounce box vanilla Jello pudding and pie filling

⅓ cup peanut butter
⅔ cup powdered sugar
2 egg whites
2 teaspoons white sugar

Make pudding as directed on box. Cool. Mix peanut butter and powdered sugar together reserving enough of mixture to sprinkle on top of pie. Mix balance of peanut butter mixture with cooled pudding and pour into pie shell. Make meringue by beating the egg whites until they form stiff peaks; mix in the sugar. Spread meringue on top of pie and sprinkle with reserved sugar and peanut butter mixture. Brown in 325 degree oven. Cool and refrigerate until time to serve.

Molly Park
Livingston County (Howell)

DELICIOUS PIE

20 graham crackers
½ cup butter, melted
⅓ cup butter
1 cup powdered sugar

1 egg
1 cup heavy cream
1 8-ounce can crushed pineapple, drained

Crush graham crackers and roll finely with a rolling pin. Add melted butter and line a pie plate with the crumbs, reserving ½ cup for topping. Do not butter the pie tin. Cream the butter, adding the sugar gradually. Then add the unbeaten egg and beat until creamy. Drop by spoonfuls onto the crumbs and smooth to a layer without mixing with the crumbs. Whip cream stiff, fold in well-drained pineapple and spread on top. Put remaining crumbs on top and refrigerate for 6 hours.

Mrs. Oren Purdy (Lee)
Gratiot County (Alma)

PINEAPPLE ANGEL PIE

1 cup crushed pineapple
1 cup pineapple juice or water
1 cup sugar
6 tablespoons cornstarch
⅓ cup cold water

3 egg whites
¼ teaspoon salt
2 tablespoons sugar
½ pint whipping cream

Combine pineapple, pineapple juice and sugar; bring to a boil. Add cornstarch that has been mixed with the water. Continue cooking until thick and clear, stirring constantly. Let cool. Beat egg whites with salt until creamy. Add the sugar and continue beating until egg whites stand in peaks. Fold into cooled pineapple mixture. Pour into baked cooled pie shell. Top with whipped cream.

Mrs. John J. Sullivan (Jean)
Monroe County (La Salle)

FROZEN PUMPKIN PIE

1 9-inch graham cracker pie crust
1 quart vanilla ice cream, softened
½ cup canned pumpkin

½ cup brown sugar, packed
½ teaspoon salt
½ teaspoon cinnamon
½ teaspoon ginger
¼ teaspoon nutmeg

In a large mixing bowl, cut up ice cream to soften. Mix pumpkin, sugar, salt and spices and fold into softened ice cream. Pour into pie shell and freeze.

Mattie Eisenlohr
Oceana County (Hart)

Desserts

PUMPKIN PIE

2 10-inch pie shells
2 cups sugar
1 teaspoon salt
3 teaspoons cinnamon
1 teaspoon nutmeg
1 teaspoon ginger
1 teaspoon allspice

1 teaspoon cloves
1 1 pound 13 ounce can Libby's pumpkin
2 13-ounce cans Carnation evaporated milk
4 eggs

Mix all ingredients until smooth. Pour in two 10-inch pie shells and bake at 425 degrees for 15 minutes or at 350 degrees for 35 minutes.

Vivian M. Wells
Kalkaska County (Kalkaska)

PUMPKIN CHIFFON PIE

1 envelope unflavored gelatin
¾ cup sugar, divided
1 teaspoon cinnamon
½ teaspoon ginger
⅔ cup evaporated milk

½ teaspoon salt
½ teaspoon nutmeg
⅛ teaspoon ground cloves
3 eggs, separated
1¼ cups canned pumpkin

Combine gelatin, ½ cup sugar, cinnamon, salt, nutmeg, ginger and cloves in saucepan. Stir in evaporated milk and egg yolks. Blend well. Place over low heat and cook, stirring constantly until gelatin dissolves and mixture thickens (about 3 minutes). Remove from heat and stir in pumpkin. Chill, stirring occasionally until mixture mounds when dropped from a spoon (about 1 hour). Beat egg whites until stiff, but not dry and gradually add remaining ¼ cup sugar. Fold in whites and put in baked pie shell. Chill overnight if possible. Top with whipped cream, if desired. *Note: May be made a day ahead!*

Mrs. Don Lund (Betty)
Washtenaw County (Ann Arbor)

CHURCH WINDOWS

1 12-ounce package chocolate chips
½ cup margarine
1 cup walnuts, chopped
1 10-ounce package miniature marshmallows
1 7-ounce package coconut

Melt chocolate chips, margarine and cool well. Add walnuts and marshmallows. Divide in ½ and form into 2 rolls. Roll in coconut and wrap in waxed paper. Cool in refrigerator for 24 hours. Slice and serve. Yield: 2 rolls.

Mrs. Ed Angove (Barb)
Emmet County (Petoskey)

BROWNIES

2 squares unsweetened chocolate
1 stick butter
1 cup sugar
⅓ cup all-purpose flour, sifted
2 eggs
1 teaspoon vanilla
1 teaspoon lemon juice

Melt chocolate. Cream butter and sugar. Add eggs to butter mixture. Add the following ingredients, mixing well after each addition: flour, melted chocolate and vanilla and lemon juice. Pour into greased 8x8x2-inch pan and bake at 350 degrees for 25 minutes. Do *not* overbake. Sift confectioners' sugar over top of brownies.

Mrs. Jerome C. Hirsch (Nancy)
Oakland County (Birmingham)

SUNDAY-BEST GINGERBREAD

1 cup hot coffee
⅓ cup shortening
1 cup molasses
½ cup sugar
1 egg, beaten
2¾ cups flour
1 teaspoon soda
⅛ teaspoon salt
1 teaspoon ginger
1 teaspoon allspice
½ cup miniature marshmallows
½ cup semi-sweet chocolate morsels
½ cup walnuts, chopped

Add hot coffee to shortening and stir until shortening melts. Add molasses and sugar, stirring until sugar dissolves. Add beaten egg. Mix and sift flour, baking soda, salt and spices. Add marshmallows, walnuts and chocolate morsels. Combine with molasses mixture. Bake in greased 8-inch square pan at 325 degrees for 1 hour. Cut into 9 squares to serve. *Note: Excellent when served warm with whipped cream.*

Lois Bransdorfer
Gratiot County (St. Louis)

MAPLE NUT COOKIES

1 stick margarine, softened
1 cup sugar
1 egg
½ teaspoon soda
2 cups flour
½ cup buttermilk or ½ cup sweet milk plus 1 tablespoon white vinegar
½ teaspoon vanilla
½ teaspoon maple flavoring
⅓ cup walnuts, chopped

Cream margarine and sugar. Add egg and beat mixture thoroughly. Add soda to flour. Then add flour and milk alternately to the sugar-margarine mixture. Next add vanilla and maple flavoring and nuts. Drop by teaspoonfuls onto a greased cookie sheet and bake at 350 degrees for 10 to 12 minutes until edge of cookie turns a light brown. *Note: This is a good basic recipe. Raisins can be substituted for nuts or you can make colored cookies and add various flavors for tea cookies. Add a dab of frosting on top of the cookies.*

DeLoris Anderson
Wexford County (Cadillac)

. . . For browner cookies, use a shiny cookie sheet.

APPLE WALNUT GOODIES (NO BAKE)

1 cup canned applesauce
1½ cups sugar
½ cup butter or margarine
¼ cup cocoa
¼ teaspoon salt
3 cups quick oatmeal
1 cup walnuts, chopped
½ teaspoon almond extract
½ teaspoon vanilla extract

Simmer applesauce gently for 5 minutes in a saucepan. Add sugar, butter, cocoa and salt. Boil for 1 minute. Remove from heat and immediately add oatmeal, walnuts, almond and vanilla extract. Mix well. Drop by teaspoonfuls onto waxed paper. When cool, roll in powdered sugar. Yield: 50 to 55 cookies or candy—you decide.

Mrs. Kenneth Dickinson (Helen)
St. Clair County (Port Huron)

AUNT JENNIE'S REFRIGERATOR COOKIES

2 sticks margarine
1 cup sugar
1 cup brown sugar
2 eggs, well beaten
1 teaspoon vanilla

1 teaspoon soda
1 teaspoon salt
4 level cups flour
1 cup nuts, chopped (Optional)

Cream margarine and sugars. Add beaten eggs and beat thoroughly. Add vanilla. Mix together soda, salt and flour. Add to above ingredients. Add nuts last and mix with hands very well. Form into a roll and refrigerate overnight. Slice and place on ungreased cookie sheet. Bake at 350 degrees for 10 to 12 minutes.

Mrs. Ernest Chamberlin (Elaine)
Cheboygan County (Topinabee)

STUFFED DATE DROPS

1 pound pitted dates (about 70)
1 3-ounce package pecan or walnut halves
¼ cup shortening
¾ cup medium brown sugar
1 egg

1¼ cups enriched flour, sifted
½ teaspoon baking powder
½ teaspoon soda
¼ teaspoon salt
½ cup sour cream

Stuff dates with nut halves. Cream shortening and sugar until light and beat in egg. Sift flour, baking powder, soda and salt and add alternately with sour cream to creamed mixture. Stir in dates and drop onto greased cookie sheet (one date per cookie). Bake at 400 degrees for 8 to 10 minutes. Cool and top with Golden Frosting.

Golden Frosting:
½ cup butter or margarine
3 cups powdered sugar, sifted

¾ teaspoon vanilla
3 tablespoons water

Lightly brown butter or margarine. Remove from heat and gradually beat in powdered sugar and vanilla. Slowly add water until frosting is spreading consistency. Yield: 5½ dozen cookies.

Mrs. Sally Beers
Huron County (Sebewaing)

Desserts

DATE DROP COOKIES

4 tablespoons boiling water
½ pound dates, chopped
1 cup shortening
1 cup brown sugar
½ cup white sugar
2 eggs, beaten

3 cups flour
½ teaspoon salt
1 teaspoon soda
1 cup walnut meats, coarsely chopped

Pour boiling water over chopped dates and set aside. Cream shortening and sugars. Then add 2 beaten eggs. Sift together flour, salt and soda. Add to mixture. Add dates that have been soaking in boiling water, nutmeats and mix well. Drop by teaspoonfuls onto greased cookie sheet. Bake at 350 degrees for 12 minutes. Yield: 5 dozen.

Twila LaBonville
Gratiot County (Wheeler)

HOLIDAY FRUIT DROPS

2 squares unsweetened chocolate
1½ cups flour, sifted
¼ teaspoon salt
¼ teaspoon baking soda
1 8-ounce package pitted chopped dates
½ pound mixed candied fruit, cubed

1 cup nuts, coarsely chopped
2 tablespoons brandy
½ cup butter or margarine, softened
1 cup brown sugar, firmly packed
1 egg
1 teaspoon vanilla extract
½ cup buttermilk

Melt chocolate over hot water; let cool. Sift flour with salt and baking soda and set aside. Lightly toss dates with candied fruit, chopped nuts, and brandy. In large bowl, beat butter, brown sugar, egg, and vanilla until smooth and fluffy. Add chocolate, beating until combined. With a wooden spoon, stir in buttermilk, then flour mixture, blending well. Stir in fruit-nut mixture and refrigerate dough, covered for 1 hour. Preheat oven to 375 degrees. Drop dough by teaspoonfuls 2 inches apart on lightly greased cookie sheets. Bake cookies 10 to 12 minutes and remove to wire rack to cool. Yield: 6 dozen.

Mrs. George Bennett (Louise)
Clinton County (Elsie)

HOLIDAY FRUIT COOKIES

1 cup Crisco
2 cups brown sugar, packed
2 eggs
½ cup sour milk or buttermilk
3½ cups flour, sifted
1 teaspoon soda
1 teaspoon salt
1½ cups pecans or walnuts, broken
2 cups candied cherries
2 cups dates, cut up

Mix together shortening, sugar and eggs. Stir in the sour milk or buttermilk. Sift together flour, soda and salt. Mix pecans or walnuts, cherries and dates and combine all mixtures. Chill at least 1 hour or overnight if possible. Drop by small teaspoonfuls about 2 inches apart onto cookie sheet. Bake 8 to 10 minutes at 400 degrees.

Mrs. Edna Cooley
Shiawassee County (Corunna)

LEMON SQUARES

2 cups flour
1 cup shortening (part butter)
½ cup powdered sugar
4 eggs
6 tablespoons lemon juice
6 tablespoons flour
2 cups sugar
1 cup coconut
1 teaspoon baking powder

Mix flour, shortening and powdered sugar. Pat in a greased 12x15-inch pan. Bake at 350 degrees for 10 minutes. Beat eggs well and add lemon juice, flour, sugar, coconut and baking powder. Mix well and pour over baked crust. Return to oven for 25 more minutes. Cool and frost. When ready to serve, cut in squares. Serves 16 to 18 depending on the size of the squares.

Frosting:
2 cups powdered sugar
½ cup soft butter
2 tablespoons hot water
2 tablespoons cold water
1 teaspoon vanilla

Mix powdered sugar, butter, hot and cold water and vanilla. Beat for 10 minutes spread on baked squares.

Mrs. Charles W. Bolender (Frances)
St. Joseph County (Centerville)

Desserts

LEMON BARS

½ cup margarine or butter
1 cup flour
½ cup powdered sugar
2 eggs

1 cup sugar
3 tablespoons fresh lemon juice
2 tablespoons flour
½ teaspoon baking powder

Cream butter, flour and powdered sugar together. Spread in 8x8-inch pan and bake at 350 degrees until very light brown, approximately 8 minutes. Beat eggs with sugar, lemon juice, flour and baking powder. Pour over crust and continue baking another 25 minutes. When cool, sprinkle with powdered sugar and cut in squares.

Florence Powers
Cass County (Dowagiac)

. . . To keep your meringue from falling, beat a little cornstarch into the egg white along with the powdered sugar.

HERMIT OATMEAL COOKIES

¾ cup margarine or butter
1 cup brown sugar, firmly
  packed
½ cup granulated sugar
2 eggs
⅓ cup milk
1 teaspoon vanilla
2 cups all-purpose flour

1 teaspoon baking soda
½ teaspoon salt
1 teaspoon cloves
¼ teaspoon nutmeg
1½ cups quick cooking oatmeal
½ cup walnuts, chopped
1 cup raisins

Cream together butter or oleo, brown sugar and granulated sugar. Beat in until well blended the eggs, milk and vanilla. Sift together flour, baking soda, salt, cloves and nutmeg. Add flour mixture to sugar mixture and mix well. Stir in oatmeal, walnuts and raisins. Drop by rounded tablespoonfuls on ungreased cookie sheets. Bake in preheated 375 degree oven for 10 to 12 minutes. Remove to wire rack to cool. Yield: 3½ dozen cookies. *Note: Make sure cookies are placed well apart on cookie sheet as they will expand.*

Marcia Fisher
Kent County (Greenville)

FESTIVE MINT BARS

Crust:
½ cup butter or margarine
½ cup sugar
6 tablespoons cocoa
1 teaspoon vanilla
1 egg, beaten
2 cups graham cracker crumbs
1 cup coconut
½ cup nuts, chopped

Mix butter, sugar, cocoa, vanilla and egg and heat in double boiler until thick. Add graham cracker crumbs, coconut and chopped nuts. Mix together well and pat into a 9x13-inch buttered loaf pan. Place in refrigerator to set while preparing filling.

Filling:
½ cup butter or margarine
3 tablespoons milk
2 tablespoons instant vanilla pudding
2 cups powdered sugar
2 to 3 drops green food coloring
½ teaspoon mint flavoring

Cream butter in medium-size bowl. In a cup, mix milk with vanilla pudding. Add to creamed butter. Gradually add powdered sugar. Beat until smooth, adding mint flavoring and green coloring to the color and taste effect you desire. Spread filling on top of chilled chocolate mixture and return to refrigerator.

Frosting:
4 ounces chocolate chips melted with 1 tablespoon butter or 1 giant plain or almond chocolate bar

Melt chocolate chips with butter or melt chocolate bar in double boiler. Spread on top of chilled filling and return to refrigerator. You may also use a chocolate powdered sugar frosting you make for cake or a canned frosting if you desire. This is an unbaked bar that yields approximately 5 dozen bars. *Note: You may leave out the green coloring and mint flavoring and you have a vanilla layered bar.*

Mrs. Henry Porras, Jr.
Menominee County (Wallace)

... Chill drop cookie dough to prevent dough from spreading.

BANANA OATMEAL DROP COOKIES

1 cup flour
¾ cup sugar
1 teaspoon baking soda
½ teaspoon cinnamon
½ teaspoon salt

2 cups oatmeal
3 tablespoons evaporated milk
1 egg
½ cup bananas, mashed
½ cup shortening, softened

Mix flour, sugar, baking soda, cinnamon, salt and oatmeal. Add evaporated milk, egg and shortening. Mix well. Blend in bananas last. Bake at 400 degrees for 10 minutes. Yield: 2½ dozen.

Gonzie Cardenas
Branch County (Coldwater)

O. HENRY BARS

4 cups quick oatmeal
1 cup brown sugar
⅔ cup butter, melted
3 teaspoons vanilla

½ cup Karo syrup
6 ounces chocolate chips
⅔ cup chunky peanut butter

Combine oatmeal and brown sugar; mix well. Add butter, vanilla and Karo to oatmeal mixture. Mix together well and pat into a 9x13-inch pan. Bake at 375 degrees for 12 minutes. Melt chocolate chips and peanut butter and spread over the cooled crust.

Mrs. Herbert Biermann (Karen)
Gladwin County (Gladwin)

OATMEAL CRISPIES COOKIES

1 cup shortening
1 cup brown sugar
1 cup white sugar
2 eggs, beaten
1 teaspoon vanilla

1 teaspoon salt
1 teaspoon soda
3 cups quick cooking oatmeal
½ cup nutmeats, chopped
1½ cups flour

Thoroughly cream shortening and sugars; add eggs and vanilla beating well. Add sifted flour, salt and soda. Add oatmeal and nutmeats; mix well. Shape into rolls; wrap in waxed paper and chill thoroughly. Slice in ¼-inch slices and bake at 350 degrees for 12 to 15 minutes. Yield: 5 dozen.

Alice M. Stuart
Lapeer County (Lapeer)

OATMEAL-JAM BARS

2 cups oatmeal
1 cup brown sugar
1 cup butter, melted
2 cups flour, sifted
½ teaspoon soda
1 teaspoon salt
1 cup jam

Mix oatmeal and sugar together. Combine with melted butter and mix well. Sift flour, soda, and salt together. Add to oatmeal mixture and stir until well blended. Mixture will be stiff. Line a greased 10x6-inch pan with ½ of mixture pressing in place. Spread jam on top. Press the remaining mixture over top and bake at 350 degrees about 30 minutes. Cut into squares when cool.

Letha E. Cunningham
Kalkaska County (Kalkaska)

. . . Use powdered sugar on your board instead of flour when rolling cookie dough. This keeps the cookies from getting tough.

KRUSTIE

4 cups flour
⅔ cup sugar
¾ teaspoon salt
⅓ cup butter, melted
8 eggs, beaten
1 quart salad oil
1 pound powdered sugar

Mix flour, sugar and salt. Cut in butter with blender. Add eggs. Dough will be quite sticky. Place the equivalent of a scant cup of dough on a heavily floured board and knead until dough can be handled and rolled out to about ¼-inch thickness. With knife, cut into 1½ to 2-inch strips, then cut each strip diagonally into about 4-inch strips, slit about an inch in the middle, tie by pulling one end through the slit. After all the dough has been rolled, cut and tied, place tied Krustie on paper towels on cookie sheet. Be sure to shake off excess flour before tying. Next, heat 2-inches depth of salad oil in a large frying pan on high heat and fry Krusties, turning to brown on both sides. Remove onto paper towels and when all are fried, dust with powdered sugar. Will produce about 3 dozen Krusties. *Note: Can be kept indefinitely in tightly covered container.*

Mary A. Lukas
Branch County (Quincy)

Desserts

CHEWY NOELS

2 tablespoons butter
⅛ teaspoon baking soda
1 cup brown sugar
2 eggs

5 tablespoons flour
1 cup nuts, chopped
1 teaspoon vanilla
Powdered sugar

Melt butter in a square pan. In bowl mix baking soda, brown sugar, eggs, flour, chopped nuts and vanilla. Mix well and pour over butter in pan. Bake at 350 degrees for 20 minutes. Invert onto waxed paper or cooling rack and sift powdered sugar over top. Cool and cut into squares. *Note: So easy and so good!*

June Odom
Eaton County (Charlotte)

POTATO CHIP COOKIES

1 cup shortening
1 cup brown sugar
1 cup white sugar
2 eggs
2 cups flour
½ teaspoon salt

1 teaspoon soda
1 teaspoon vanilla
2 cups potato chips, slightly crushed
1 cup nutmeats

Cream shortening and sugars. Add eggs, vanilla and cream well. Add flour, salt and soda. Stir well. Add potato chips and nuts. Drop onto ungreased cookie sheet. Bake at 350 degrees for 12 minutes. Yield: 7 dozen. *Note: These are delicious and help to use up stale or broken potato chips.*

Lillian McLean
Clare County (Harrison)

DIABETIC SUGARLESS ORANGE COOKIES

½ cup soft margarine
1 egg
½ cup freshly squeezed orange juice
2 cups flour

2 teaspoons baking powder
½ teaspoon cinnamon
½ teaspoon salt
½ cup nuts, chopped
½ cup seedless raisins

Mix margarine, egg and orange juice. Add flour, baking powder, cinnamon, salt, nuts and raisins. Drop by teaspoonfuls onto cookie sheet and bake at 375 degrees for 20 minutes. *Note: These cookies are especially made for diabetics to eat. Two cookies equal 60 calories (½ fruit exchange and ½ fat exchange).*

Leone G. Stamman
Clare County (Harrison)

PERFECT RAISIN COOKIES

2 cups raisins
1 cup water
1 teaspoon soda
1 cup shortening
2 cups sugar
3 eggs, well beaten
4 cups all-purpose flour, sifted
1 teaspoon baking powder
1 teaspoon salt
1 teaspoon cinnamon
¼ teaspoon nutmeg
1 teaspoon vanilla
1 cup nutmeats (Optional)

Boil raisins in water for 5 minutes. Cool. Stir in soda. Cream shortening and sugar. Add well beaten eggs and vanilla. Mix well. Add raisins with the soda mixture and add nuts. Add sifted flour with baking powder and spices. Beat well. Drop by spoonfuls onto greased baking sheet. Bake at 350 degrees for 10 to 12 minutes.

Mrs. Reuben Pruetz (Edna)
Bay County (Bay City)

PUMPKIN SQUARES

Crust:
1 cup flour
½ cup oatmeal
½ cup brown sugar
½ cup butter or oleo

Combine ingredients until crumbly. Press into ungreased 13x9x2-inch pan. Bake at 350 degrees for 15 minutes.

Filling:
2 cups pumpkin
1 can evaporated milk
2 eggs
¾ cup sugar
½ teaspoon cinnamon
½ teaspoon ginger
¼ teaspoon cloves

Combine all filling ingredients and beat well. Pour over baked crust. Return to oven for 20 minutes at 350 degrees.

Topping:
½ cup pecans, chopped
½ cup brown sugar, packed
2 tablespoons butter

Blend topping ingredients until crumbly—sprinkle over pumpkin filling. Finish baking at 350 degrees for 15 to 20 minutes or until set.

Mrs. Albert Wrisley
Leelanau County (Northport Pointe)

BANANA SPLIT DESSERT

½ stick margarine, melted
2 cups graham cracker crumbs
2 eggs
2 sticks butter
2 cups powdered sugar
4 or more bananas, sliced
1 No. 2 can crushed pineapple, drained
1 large carton Cool Whip
½ cup pecans, chopped
¼ cup Maraschino cherries, chopped

Combine melted margarine and graham cracker crumbs. Pat into bottom of 9x13-inch pan. Beat eggs, butter and sugar for 15 minutes. Spread over crust. Arrange bananas over egg mixture. Cover with layer of pineapple and top with Cool Whip. Sprinkle with chopped pecans and decorate with cherries. Refrigerate severals hours or overnight. Yield: 15 servings.

Mrs. Harold H. Mammel (Ruth)
Huron County (Sebewaing)

Betty Ann Schneider
Marquette County (Marquette)

DANISH PASTRY

1 cup flour
½ cup margarine
2 tablespoons water

Heat oven to 350 degrees. Cut flour into margarine and add water. Form a ball of dough and divide in ½. Pat dough into two 12x3-inch strips on an ungreased cookie sheet. Spread ½ of filling over each strip. Bake 1 hour and frost with powdered sugar frosting flavored with almond flavoring. Sprinkle with sliced almonds.

Filling:
½ cup margarine
1 cup water
1 teaspoon almond flavoring
1 cup flour
3 eggs

Boil margarine and water in saucepan. Add almond flavoring and flour quickly. Remove from heat. Add egg one at a time, beating after each addition.

Helene A. Leach
Ottawa County (Holland)

BUTTERSCOTCH TORTE

6 eggs, separated
1½ cups sugar
1 teaspoon baking powder
2 teaspoons vanilla
1 teaspoon almond extract
2 cups graham cracker crumbs
1 cup nuts, chopped

Beat egg yolks well. Slowly add sugar, baking powder and flavorings. Mix well. Beat egg whites until they hold stiff peaks; fold into yolk mixture. Fold in crumbs and nuts. Pour into two 9-inch layer pans, greased and lined with waxed paper. Bake at 325 degrees for 30 to 35 minutes. Cool 10 minutes then remove from pans. Frost when completely cooled. Serves 12.

Frosting:
2 cups heavy cream
3 tablespoons powdered sugar

Whip cream, slowly adding powdered sugar. Spread between layers and over top and sides of torte. *Note: You may substitute 1 large carton of whipped topping for Frosting.*

Sauce:
¼ cup water
¼ cup butter, melted
1 cup brown sugar
1 tablespoon flour
1 egg, well beaten
¼ cup orange juice
½ teaspoon vanilla

In saucepan, add water and margarine. Blend in brown sugar and flour. Add juice, egg and vanilla. Mix well and bring to boil. Cook until thickened. Cool thoroughly and pour over frosted torte so the sauce drizzles down the sides.

Joyce Short
Gratiot County (Breckenridge)

. . . Mix 3 or 4 marbles with your candy ingredients to keep candy from burning or scalding. The boiling syrup keeps them in motion and they stir the mixture from the bottom.

RHUBARB CRUNCH

1 cup flour
¾ cup oatmeal
½ cup butter or margarine, melted
1 cup brown sugar
¾ teaspoon cinnamon

6 cups rhubarb, diced
1½ cups sugar
3 tablespoons cornstarch
1½ cups water
1 teaspoon vanilla

Combine flour and oatmeal in mixing bowl. Stir in butter, brown sugar and cinnamon until crumbly. Put ¾ of crumbs in 13x9-inch cake pan and pack down to make crust. Add 6 cups of raw rhubarb over crust. In saucepan, cook sugar, cornstarch and water together boiling until thick. Add vanilla to thickening and pour over rhubarb. Sprinkle remainder of crumb mixture on top. Bake at 350 degrees for 1 hour. *Note: You can substitute apples for rhubarb.*

Marilyn J. Hamilton
Ogemaw County (West Branch)

... Want a different tasting brownie recipe? Add 4 crushed peppermints sticks to batter.

PISTACHIO DESSERT

1 box Jello Instant pistachio pudding and pie filling
1 9-ounce carton Cool Whip
1 20 to 22-ounce can crushed pineapple, undrained and chilled

1 cup miniature marshmallows
½ cup nuts, chopped (Optional)

Pour the pistachio pudding and pie filling into the already whipped Cool Whip. Add the chilled, undrained pineapple and whip again. Add the marshmallows and mix thoroughly. Add the nuts last (if desired). *Note: This dessert can be used immediately and can be kept refrigerated for future use for a couple of days.*

Cleo Meyerhofer
Wexford County (Cadillac)

FOUR LAYER DESSERT

First Layer:
1 cup flour
½ stick margarine
½ cup walnuts, chopped

Combine ingredients and press into a lightly greased 9x13-inch pan. Bake at 375 degrees for 15 minutes. Cool.

Second Layer:
1 8-ounce package cream cheese
1 cup powdered sugar
1 cup Cool Whip (reserve rest of large carton)
¾ cup crushed pineapple, well drained

Mix together and spread over cooled crust.

Third Layer:
2 packages instant vanilla pudding
3 cups cold milk

Mix together and spread over Second Layer.

Fourth Layer:
Reserved Cool Whip
Chopped nuts

Cover with remainder of large size carton of Cool Whip (see Second Layer) and sprinkle with chopped nuts.

Darlene Wood
Montmorency County (Hillman)

HOT FUDGE SAUCE

½ pound butter
1 pound powdered sugar
¼ pound unsweetened baking chocolate
¼ pound sweet baking chocolate
1 13-ounce can evaporated milk
Dash salt
1 teaspoon vanilla

In heavy 2-quart saucepan on double boiler, combine butter, sugar, chocolates and milk. Cook for 20 to 30 minutes stirring almost constantly until it thickens. Remove from heat and beat in salt and vanilla.

Mrs. Bo Schembechler (Millie)
Washtenaw County (Ann Arbor)

Desserts

LEMON DESSERT

1 cup flour
1 stick margarine
½ cup nuts, finely chopped
1 8-ounce package cream cheese, softened
1 cup powdered sugar

1 4-cup container Cool Whip, divided in half
3 cups milk
2 packages instant lemon pudding
Grated rind of lemon

Mix flour, margarine and nuts and press in 9x13-inch pan. Bake at 350 degrees for 15 minutes and cool. Mix cream cheese, powdered sugar and 2 cups Cool Whip thoroughly and spread over pastry. Mix 3 cups milk with lemon pudding and pour over cream cheese mixture. Top with remaining 2 cups Cool Whip and sprinkle with grated rind of lemon if desired. Serves 15.

Mrs. Robert Gorno (Ada)
Monroe County (Ida)

MOCHA PECAN FUDGE

1 cup sugar
4 teaspoons instant coffee
1 ¾-ounce package chocolate pudding and pie filling mix (not instant)

½ cup evaporated milk
1 tablespoon butter or margarine
1 cup pecans, chopped

Blend sugar and coffee with pudding mix in a heavy saucepan. Stir in evaporated milk. Add butter or margarine. Cook and stir over medium heat until mixture boils. Boil 4 minutes to thicken. Remove from heat, stir in chopped pecans and beat until candy thickens further. Pour into a buttered 9x5-inch loaf pan; spread evenly. Cool and cut into squares. Yield: 1¼ pounds fudge. *Note: Walnuts may be substituted for pecans.*

Mrs. Kenneth Dickinson (Helen)
St. Clair County (Port Huron)

BAKED RICE PUDDING

1 cup regular white rice, uncooked
1⅔ cups evaporated milk
1¼ cups water
¼ teaspoon salt
⅛ teaspoon nutmeg
2 tablespoons margarine
1 teaspoon vanilla extract
½ cup brown sugar

Combine all ingredients in 1½-quart casserole dish. Mix well; cover and bake at 325 degrees for 1½ to 2 hours or until liquid is absorbed and rice is tender. Serves 6.

Mrs. Garnet Tripp
Montmorency County (Hillman)

... Sift powdered sugar on your cake plate before placing fresh cake on it to keep it from sticking.

TAYLOR DUFF

1 egg
2 tablespoons sugar
½ teaspoon salt
½ cup light molasses
2 tablespoons butter, melted
1 teaspoon soda dissolved in ¼ cup hot water
1½ cups flour, sifted
½ cup boiling water

Beat egg and add sugar and salt. Beat in molasses in melted butter. Add soda water and beat in sifted flour. Add boiling water. Place in buttered small bundt pan over cold water and steam for 1 hour. *Note: It is important that you do not remove cover from mold while steaming.*

Sauce:
3 egg yolks
1 teaspoon vanilla
½ cup powdered sugar
1 pint whipping cream, whipped

Mix egg yolks, vanilla and sugar. Add whipped cream before serving. Spoon over sliced individual servings of Taylor Duff.

Jane Schermerhorn
Special Writer, Detroit News
Wayne County (Detroit)

CHOCOLATE ICE BOX DESSERT

1 12-ounce package
  chocolate chips
4 tablespoons sugar
6 eggs, separated

2 cups whipping cream
2 teaspoons vanilla
1 teaspoon salt
Angel food cake

Line flat 9x9-inch cake pan with waxed paper. Slice angel food cake and place a layer of cake in cake pan. (I find that angel food cake slices better if frozen.) Beat egg yolks. Melt chocolate chips in a double boiler or over water, and add sugar and water. Mix well making sure sugar melts. Remove from heat and combine hot chocolate mixture gradually into the beaten yolks. Beat until smooth. Cool chocolate mixture. Add vanilla and salt and mix. Beat the egg whites until stiff; whip whipping cream. Fold egg whites into the cooled chocolate mixture, then the whipping cream. Place a layer of the chocolate mixture on the sliced angel food cake, then another layer of cake, then a layer of chocolate. Place in refrigerator and chill overnight. This may be frozen and used later. Be sure to chill overnight before freezing.

Mrs. Gerald R. Ford (Betty)

Michigan Fruit Basket

Fruit Basket

FRESH APPLE CAKE

2½ cups flour
1 teaspoon baking soda
1 teaspoon baking powder
½ teaspoon salt
2 teaspoons cinnamon
¾ cup margarine

1 cup white sugar
1 cup brown sugar
2 eggs
1 cup sour milk
2 cups raw apples, chopped and peeled

Combine flour, baking soda, baking powder, salt and cinnamon together and set aside. Cream margarine and sugars. Add eggs and sour milk to sugar mixture. Add dry ingredients and mix well. Stir in apples. Pour batter into greased 9x13-inch pan. Sprinkle topping over batter and bake at 375 degrees for 40 to 45 minutes.

Topping:
¼ cup white sugar
¼ cup nuts, chopped

1 teaspoon cinnamon

Mix topping ingredients together and sprinkle over batter before baking.

Mrs. Robert Ptaszenski
Mason County (Ludington)

IVA LANE'S APPLE CAKE

1 cup oil
1½ cups sugar
2 eggs
2 cups flour
1 teaspoon salt

1 teaspoon soda
3 cups apples, chopped
1 cup coconut, flaked
½ cup nutmeats

Mix oil and sugar well. Add eggs and mix thoroughly. Combine flour, salt and soda and add by one-thirds to first mixture. Add apples, coconut and nutmeats and mix thoroughly by hand. Place in greased 9x13-inch pan and bake at 350 degrees for 30 to 40 minutes. Frost when cooled. Serves 15 to 20.

Frosting:
4 ounces cream cheese
2 cups powdered sugar

¼ cup butter or margarine
1 teaspoon vanilla

Beat all ingredients together. Frost cooled cake.

Mrs. Thomas Buskard (Iva Lane)
Ottawa County (Marne)

NOBBY APPLE CAKE

2 tablespoons butter or
   margarine
1 cup sugar
1 egg, beaten
½ teaspoon cinnamon
½ teaspoon nutmeg

½ teaspoon salt
1 teaspoon baking soda
1 cup flour, sifted
3 cups apples, diced
¼ cup nuts, chopped
1 teaspoon vanilla

Cream butter and sugar; add egg and mix well. Sift cinnamon, nutmeg, salt, baking soda and flour. Stir in diced apples, nuts and vanilla. Use Cortland or other apple that holds it shape in cooking. Pour into greased 8x8x2-inch pan. Bake at 350 degrees for 40 to 45 minutes. Serve hot or cold. *Note: Whipped cream or ice cream make an excellent topping for this cake!*

Fern Hawes
Alcona County (Barton City)

TRAVELIN' CAKE

3 eggs
2 cups sugar
1 cup butter
½ cup water
2½ cups flour
2 tablespoons cocoa
1 teaspoon cinnamon

1 teaspoon allspice
½ teaspoon salt
2 cups fresh apples, grated
1 cup nuts, chopped
¾ cup chocolate chips
¾ cup raisins (Optional)
1 teaspoon vanilla

Cream together eggs, sugar, butter and water. Sift flour with cocoa, soda, cinnamon, allspice and salt. Mix well into creamed mixture. Fold in apples, nuts, chocolate chips, raisins and vanilla. Bake in greased and floured tube pan at 325 degrees for 60 to 70 minutes until cake tester comes out clean. Cool for 15 minutes in pan, then turn out onto wire rack. *Note: Even a week in the mail does not spoil this cake. Your young people away at school will call you blessed if you send this cake to them!*

Dorothea Kearney
Ingham County (East Lansing)

. . . Be sure to prick the skins of baking apples so the apples will cook without bursting.

Fruit Basket

APPLE STREUSEL

6 to 8 apples (2 pounds), pared and sliced
4 tablespoons sugar
½ scant teaspoon cinnamon
1 cup flour
½ cup butter or margarine
½ cup brown sugar

Arrange apple slices in a generously buttered 8x12-inch pan. Mix 4 tablespoons sugar and cinnamon; sprinkle over apples. Put flour and brown sugar in a bowl; cut in butter or margarine and rub with your fingertips to crumbs. Sprinkle crumb mixture over and between the apples and pat to a smooth surface. Bake at 400 degrees for 30 minutes. *Note: Serve with ice cream or whipped topping.*

Mrs. Ernest Lucas (Grace)
Oscoda County (Mio)

APPLESAUCE PUFFS

2 cups packaged biscuit mix
¼ cup sugar
1 teaspoon cinnamon
½ cup applesauce
¼ cup milk
1 egg, slightly beaten
2 tablespoons oil
¼ cup sugar
¼ teaspoon cinnamon
2 tablespoons butter or margarine, melted

Combine biscuit mix, ¼ cup sugar and 1 teaspoon cinnamon. Add applesauce, milk, egg and oil. Beat vigorously for 30 seconds. Fill 2 inch muffin pans two-thirds full. Bake at 400 degrees for 12 minutes or until golden. Cool slightly; remove from pans. Mix ¼ cup sugar and ¼ teaspoon cinnamon. Dip tops of muffins in the sugar-cinnamon mixture. Yield: 24 muffins.

Mrs. Azell Van Dyke
Montmorency County (Lewiston)

COSMOPOLITAN APPLE PIE

⅓ cup granulated sugar
¼ cup brown sugar
¼ teaspoon salt
2 tablespoons flour
5 cups apples, thinly sliced
1 9-inch unbaked pie shell
⅔ cup cream
⅛ teaspoon cinnamon

Mix together sugars, salt and flour. Add sliced apples to this mixture and stir. Place apple mixture into unbaked pie shell. Pour cream over apples and sprinkle with cinnamon. Bake at 375 degrees for 50 to 60 minutes. Serve warm. *Note: Pie may be served topped with ice cream or whipped cream.*

Mrs. Frederick Strobel (Edna)
St. Joseph County (Centreville)

DUTCH APPLE DELIGHT

1 cup flour
1 teaspoon baking powder
1 teaspoon cinnamon, divided
⅓ cup margarine
½ cup packed brown sugar
1 egg

¼ cup milk
1 cup Kraft cheese, shredded
3½ cups apple slices, peeled
½ cup granulated sugar
½ cup nuts, chopped

Combine flour, baking powder and ½ teaspoon cinnamon. Cream margarine and brown sugar. Add egg and beat well. Add flour mixture to creamed mixture alternately with milk, mixing well after each addition. Stir in ½ cup cheese. Pour into greased 10x6-inch baking dish. Combine apples, sugar and remaining cinnamon. Place over batter and top with nuts. Bake at 375 degrees for 35 minutes. Top with remaining cheese. Serve with whipped cream if desired. Serves 6 to 8.

Gerry Rich
Lapeer County (Lapeer)

APPLE BREAD

½ cup shortening
1 cup white sugar
2 eggs, well beaten
2 tablespoons sour milk
1 teaspoon soda

1 teaspoon salt
2 cups flour, sifted
1 teaspoon vanilla
2 cups apples, peeled and finely chopped

Mix shortening, sugar, eggs, milk, soda, salt, flour, vanilla and apples together in large bowl. Pour batter into a 9x5x3-inch bread pan. Spread Topping over dough batter. Bake for 60 minutes in 325 degree oven. Yield: 1 loaf. *Note: Double recipe and make 3 loaves. Triple Topping.*

Topping:
2 tablespoons butter
2 tablespoons flour

1 tablespoon sugar
1 teaspoon cinnamon

Mix together all ingredients and spread over dough batter.

Maxine Jerue
Cass County (Dowagiac)

Marie Kamps
Ottawa County (Hudsonville)

Fruit Basket

DUTCH APPLE BREAD

1 cup sugar
½ cup shortening
2 eggs, beaten
2 cups flour
1 teaspoon soda
¼ teaspoon salt

1½ tablespoons sour milk
1 teaspoon orange extract
1 teaspoon vanilla
1 cup apples, chopped
½ cup nuts (Optional)

Cream sugar and shortening and add eggs. Sift flour, soda and salt and add milk. Add orange extract, vanilla, apples and nuts. Grease pans. Makes 1 large or 2 small loaves. Before baking, put mixture of 1 teaspoon cinnamon and 2 teaspoons sugar on top of loaves. Bake at 350 degrees for 1 hour. *Note: I didn't have orange extract so I substituted ¼ cup Tang powdered breakfast drink for ¼ cup of sugar.*

Mrs. Pauline Sibille
Muskegon County (Muskegon)

ELAINE'S APPLE BREAD

1 stick margarine
1 cup sugar
2 eggs
1 teaspoon baking soda
2 tablespoons milk

2 cups flour
1 teaspoon vanilla
2 cups apples, diced
½ cup nuts, chopped (Optional)

Cream margarine and sugar. Add eggs, one at a time, beating thoroughly after each addition. Dissolve baking soda in milk and add to mixture. Stir in flour and vanilla. Combine apples and nuts. Pour batter into greased 1½-quart loaf pan. Sprinkle topping evenly over batter and bake 60 minutes at 350 degrees.

Topping:
2 tablespoons flour
2 tablespoons sugar
¾ teaspoon cinnamon

Pinch salt
2 teaspoons butter or margarine, melted

Combine flour, sugar, cinnamon and salt. Melt butter and add to dry mixture using fork to make a crumbly topping.

Mrs. Jarold Groters (Elaine)
Ottawa County (Zeeland)

BROILED APPLE CRÊPES

3 medium apples, peeled, cored, chopped (3 cups)
1 tablespoon sugar
3 tablespoons cornstarch, divided
¾ teaspoon ground cinnamon
2¼ cups apple juice
12 crêpes
2 tablespoon light or dark brown sugar

In large bowl, mix together apples, sugar, 1 tablespoon of cornstarch and cinnamon; set aside. Into large saucepan, place remaining 2 tablespoons cornstarch. Gradually stir in apple juice until smooth. Stirring constantly, bring to boil over medium heat and boil 1 minute. Reserve ¾ cup sauce. To remaining sauce, add apple mixture. Stirring occasionally, cook over medium heat 5 to 10 minutes or until apples are tender. Fill crêpes with about 3 tablespoons filling each and roll up. Place crêpes in one 13x9x2-inch baking pan. Pour reserved sauce over top. Sprinkle with brown sugar. Broil 3 to 5 minutes or until bubbly. Serves 6.

Esther Kutz
Berrien County (St. Joseph)

APPLE CHEESE CRUNCH

5 medium apples, preferably Jonathan or McIntosh
½ cup sugar
1 teaspoon ground cinnamon
2 tablespoons water

Peel, core and slice apples. Place in buttered 8-inch Pyrex dish. Combine sugar and cinnamon and sprinkle over apples. Gently, sprinkle water over apples. Cover with topping. Bake at 325 degrees for 45 minutes. *Note: Use a 14x9-inch Pyrex dish if you double the recipe. Can be served hot or cold and is delicious with whipped cream topping.*

Topping:
1 cup flour
½ cup sugar
1 teaspoon sugar
1 teaspoon salt
1 cup sharp Cheddar cheese, shredded
½ cup margarine, melted

Combine flour, sugar, salt, Cheddar cheese, and melted margarine for topping and mix to crumbly consistency. Take by hand and crumble over apples evenly.

Mrs. Rita M. Eby
Monroe County (Monroe)

Fruit Basket

APPLE BARS

2 cups all-purpose flour
½ cup sugar
½ teaspoon baking powder
½ teaspoon salt
1 cup butter or margarine
2 egg yolks, beaten
4 medium apples, pared, cored and sliced (4 cups)

¾ cup sugar
¼ cup all-purpose flour
1 teaspoon ground cinnamon
1 egg white, slightly beaten (Optional)

Combine 2 cups flour, ½ cup sugar, baking powder and salt. Cut in butter or margarine until crumbs are the size of small peas. Stir in egg yolks. Divide mixture in ½. Press ½ over bottom of a 13x9x2-inch baking pan. Combine apples, remaining sugar and flour, and cinnamon; arrange over bottom crust. Crumble remaining dough over apples. Brush egg white over all if desired. Bake at 350 degrees for 40 to 45 minutes. Cool and drizzle with thin powdered sugar icing if desired. Cut into bars. Yield: 4 dozen bars.

Lydia Buckler
Antrim County (Rapid City)

. . . Muffin tins are excellent for baking apples.

APPLE CRISP

6 to 8 cups apples, sliced
½ cup water
2 teaspoons cinnamon
2 teaspoons salt

1½ cups flour, sifted
2 cups sugar
⅔ cup butter

Fill a 9x13x2-inch cake pan approximately 1½ inches from the bottom with sliced apples. Sprinkle the apples with water, cinnamon, and salt. Work together flour, sugar and butter until crumbly. Spread this crumb mixture over the apples. Bake uncovered at 350 degrees for 60 to 80 minutes. Serve warm with whipped cream or ice cream. Serves 8 to 12. *Note: Length of baking time depends on type of apples used. Recipe is baked well when crumb mixture is golden brown and the apple juice has bubbled through the crumb mixture.*

Donna J. Luczak
Bay County (Bay City)

FRESH APPLE CRISP

¼ cup sugar
½ teaspoon cloves
½ teaspoon nutmeg
¼ cup honey
4 cups apples, sliced
⅓ cup sugar
⅓ cup shortening
2 eggs
1 teaspoon vanilla
1½ cups bread cubes, toasted (4 slices bread)
1½ cups corn flakes

Combine sugar, cloves, nutmeg and honey. Add apples. Turn into greased 9x9-inch baking dish. Blend sugar, shortening, eggs and vanilla. Beat well. Mix with bread cubes and corn flakes and spread over apples. Bake at 350 degrees for 40 to 45 minutes or until apples are tender and top is brown.

Kreta Lane
Montcalm County (Greenville)

APPLE DESSERT

9 cups baking apples, sliced and peeled
½ cup sugar
1 teaspoon cinnamon
¾ cup butter
1 cup sugar
1 cup flour
1 egg
½ cup walnuts, chopped
Pinch of salt

Toss together apples, ½ cup sugar and cinnamon. Place into 3-quart greased casserole dish. Mix together butter, 1 cup sugar, flour, egg, walnuts and salt and put over apples. Bake at 350 degrees for 1 hour. *Note: Serve warm topped with vanilla ice cream or whipped cream.*

Kathleen C. Hasse
Oakland County (Farmington)

BLUEBERRY PIE

1 9-inch pie shell, baked
4 cups frozen blueberries, not thawed
1 cup sugar
1 tablespoon water
4½ tablespoons cornstarch
Pinch salt
1 tablespoon lemon juice
1 tablespoon butter
Whipped cream

In saucepan combine 2 cups frozen blueberries, sugar, water, cornstarch and salt. Cook together until very thick. Add lemon juice and cool a little. Add butter then remainder of frozen blueberries. Pour into baked 9-inch pie shell and refrigerate. *Note: Just before serving top with whipped cream. It's delicious!*

Betty Beadle
Oceana County (Hart)

Fruit Basket

BLUEBERRY CAKE

1 cup sugar
½ cup shortening
2 eggs
⅔ cup milk
1 teaspoon vanilla

2¼ cups flour
3 teaspoons baking powder
¼ teaspoon salt
2 cups fresh blueberries

Cream sugar and shortening. Add eggs and beat well. Add milk and vanilla. Beat well. Sift dry ingredients and mix well. Fold in berries and pour into a 9x12-inch pan. Sprinkle topping over batter and bake at 350 degrees for 45 minutes.

Topping:
⅓ cup sugar
⅓ cup flour

½ cup butter
¼ teaspoon almond flavoring

Using pastry cutter, mix all ingredients until crumbly. Sprinkle over blueberry cake batter.

Darleen Seiter
Clare County (Clare)

BLUEBERRY BUNDT CAKE

1 cup butter or margarine
2 cups sugar
3 eggs
½ cup milk
3 cups all-purpose flour, sifted

1½ teaspoons baking powder
⅛ teaspoon salt
¼ teaspoon mace
2 cups blueberries (1 pint), washed and dried

Cream butter and sugar well. Add egg, one at a time, blending well with each addition. Add milk alternately with sifted flour, baking powder, salt and mace. Fold in washed and dried blueberries. Pour into a greased bundt pan. Bake at 350 degrees for 1 hour and 20 minutes. Serves 12 to 15. *Note: This recipe can be used as a bread, but sugar should be reduced to 1½ cups. Wrap in Saran Wrap and store in refrigerator for 24 hours before slicing.*

Mrs. Jerry Dumar (Eleanore)
Manistee County (Manistee)

BLUEBERRY MUFFINS

½ cup margarine or butter
¾ cup white sugar
2 eggs, separated
2 cups flour
3½ teaspoons baking powder

½ teaspoon salt
1 cup milk
1 cup or more of fresh or frozen blueberries

Cream butter and sugar. Separate yolks from whites of eggs. Add yolks to butter and sugar mixture, one at a time, beating thoroughly after each addition. Measure flour before sifting. Sift together flour, baking powder and salt and add to egg mixture alternately with milk. Do not overbeat. Fold in stiffly beaten egg whites. Fill greased muffin pans barely ½ full. Cover with blueberries. Distribute berries downward through batter with blunt knife. Cover with more batter. Repeat process of adding and distributing more berries. Bake at 400 to 425 degrees for 20 minutes. Yield: 12 large muffins.

Clio VanValkenburg
Kalamazoo County (Kalamazoo)

. . . To make berry pies plump with juice, stick two 3-inch paper funnels into the crust slits. Juice will rise in the funnels during baking without emptying in oven. Remove funnels before serving.

BLUEBERRY BREAD

½ cup shortening
2 cups flour
1 tablespoon baking powder
½ teaspoon salt
1½ cups granulated sugar

1⅛ cups milk
2 eggs
1½ cups blueberries, well-drained (canned or fresh)

Cream shortening until well softened. Add flour, baking powder, salt and sugar that have been sifted together. Add milk and heat well for 2 minutes. Add eggs one at a time, beating after each addition. Stir in blueberries. Bake at 350 degrees for 45 to 50 minutes in well greased and floured loaf pans. Use 2 regular bread pans or 4 small bread pans.

Mrs. M. J. Schoendorf
Clinton County (Elsie)

Fruit Basket

CHERRY CHEWS

Pastry:
3 cups flour
1½ teaspoons salt
1 cup plus 2 tablespoons
   shortening

1 egg, separated
¾ cup milk

Blend flour and salt with pastry blender adding shortening. Beat yolk of egg with milk and add to flour mixture. Roll half of recipe on floured board and place on 12x17-inch cookie sheet. Spoon on cooled fruit mixture and cover with remaining pastry. Brush top with slightly beaten egg white. Bake at 375 degrees for 45 to 55 minutes. Serves 12 to 24.

Fruit Mixture:
6 cups cherries, slightly
   thawed
1½ cups sugar
5 tablespoons cornstarch
½ cup juice from cherries

½ teaspoon salt
2 tablespoons butter
1 teaspoon almond extract
½ teaspoon nutmeg

Cook cherries and sugar over medium heat until they begin to simmer. Mix cornstarch and juice together and add to fruit. Stir constantly and continue to simmer mixture until it becomes clear. Add salt, butter, almond extract and nutmeg. Set aside to cool and spoon on pastry.

Mrs. Edna Mae Howell
Berrien County (Galien)

CHERRY-PINEAPPLE CAKE
(Dump Cake)

1 1-pound 4-ounce can
   crushed pineapple, drained
1 can cherry pie filling
1 cup coconut

1 box yellow cake mix
2 sticks margarine, melted to
   drizzle over cake
1 cup nutmeats

Place ingredients in order given in 9x13-inch greased pan. Bake at 300 degrees for 1 hour.

Mrs. Erma Kleinhardt
Clare County (Clare)

CHERRY CHOCOLATE CAKE

1 package chocolate cake mix
3 eggs
1 21-ounce can cherry pie filling

Combine cake mix, eggs and cherry pie filling. Mix until well blended. Pour into greased and floured 9x13-inch pan. Bake at 350 degrees for 35 to 40 minutes, or until cake springs back when lightly touched. Frost when cooled.

Frosting:
1 cup sugar
3 tablespoons butter or margarine
⅓ cup milk
1 6-ounce package semi-sweet chocolate pieces

In a small saucepan combine sugar, butter and milk. Bring to a boil, stirring constantly and cook for 1 minute. Remove from heat; stir in chocolate pieces until melted and smooth. Spread over cake.

Bobbie J. Smart
Alpena County (Hillman)

... To keep bottom crust of cobblers from becoming soggy, set cobblers on a rack to cool.

MY FAVORITE COBBLER

¼ cup butter, softened
½ cup white sugar
2 teaspoons baking powder
1 cup flour
¼ teaspoon salt
½ cup milk
1 can cherries, blueberries, or peaches, drained with juice reserved
¼ to ½ cup white sugar
1 cup fruit juice

Preheat oven to 375 degrees. Cream butter and ½ cup sugar. Mix baking powder, flour and salt and add alternately with milk. Beat until smooth. Pour batter into greased 10x5x3-inch loaf pan or 2-quart casserole. Spoon fruit over batter. Sprinkle with sugar and pour juice over top. Bake at 350 degrees for 45 to 50 minutes. During baking, juice goes to bottom of cobbler and a cake-like layer forms on top. Serve warm with ice cream or whole cream. *Note: I use red food coloring for the cherries.*

Mrs. Woodrow Wilson
Montmorency County (Atlanta)

Fruit Basket

FROZEN CRANBERRY SALAD

1 pound package cranberries
1 package miniature
  marshmallows
2 cups sugar
1 No. 2 can crushed pineapple, not
  drained
1 pint whipping cream

Put cranberries through food chopper. Stir in marshmallows, sugar and pineapple. Mix well, cover and let sit at least 6 hours. Whip cream until stiff and add to first mixture. Pour in 1 large or 2 small molds and freeze overnight. *Note: About ½ cup chopped walnuts added to the whipped cream makes a nice addition. Also, Cool Whip may be substituted for the whipped cream, but is not quite as good.*

Mrs. Clarence Leppien (Dorothy)
Gratiot County (Alma)

. . . Cooking at high temperatures reduces the potency of spices.

JULIE'S FROZEN CRANBERRY SALAD

1 8-ounce package cream
  cheese
½ cup white sugar
3 teaspoons lemon juice
1 1-pound can whole berry
  cranberry sauce
½ cup nuts, chopped (Optional)
1 9-ounce carton Cool Whip,
  thawed

Cream together cream cheese and sugar until fluffy. Beat in lemon juice and fold in cranberry sauce and nuts. Fold in thawed Cool Whip and mix all well. Pour into 1-quart mold or a 9x5x3½-inch loaf pan. (I recommend spraying with Pam first.) Freeze for 24 hours. Remove from freezer just before serving. Unmold and garnish with green grapes if desired.

Carmen Golden
Monroe County (Monroe)

CRANBERRY SAUCE CAKE

3 cups flour, sifted
1½ cups sugar
1 teaspoon baking soda
1 teaspoon salt
1 1-pound can whole cranberry sauce, reserve ¼ cup

1 cup pecans, chopped
1 cup Hellman's Real Mayonnaise
2 tablespoons orange rind, grated
⅓ cup orange juice
2 tablespoons butter
2 cups powdered sugar

Sift flour, sugar, soda and salt into mixing bowl. Stir cranberry sauce (except for reserved ¼ cup), pecans, mayonnaise, orange rind and orange juice into dry ingredients. Stir well. Bake in greased 13x9x2-inch pan at 350 degrees for 45 minutes. While cake bakes, mix reserved ¼ cup cranberry sauce, butter and powdered sugar until creamy. Spread on warm cake. Serves 16.

Mrs. Joseph Hennigar (Marie)
Iosco County (East Tawas)

CRANBERRY NUT BREAD

3 cups flour, sifted
4 teaspoons baking powder
1 teaspoon salt
1 cup granulated sugar
Grated peel of 1 orange

1 egg, beaten
1 cup milk
2 tablespoons butter, melted
1½ cups cranberries, sliced
1 cup pecans, chopped

Sift together flour, baking powder, salt and sugar. Add grated orange peel. Combine egg, milk and melted butter. Gradually stir in flour mixture. Add sliced cranberries and pecans. Pour into greased and floured loaf pan. Bake at 350 degrees for 1 hour. Cool thoroughly, wrap in foil and refrigerate before slicing. *Note: This bread makes delicious sandwiches with butter or cream cheese filling.*

Kathleen C. Hasse
Oakland County (Farmington)

CRANBERRY MOUSSE WITH RASPBERRY SAUCE

3 cups fresh or fresh frozen cranberries
1 cup sugar
1 quart cranberry juice cocktail
3 envelopes unflavored gelatin
⅓ cup Kirsch or light rum (Kirsch is a cherry liqueur)
2 cups (1 pint) heavy cream, whipped

Rinse cranberries. In medium saucepan, combine cranberries, sugar and 1 cup cranberry juice. Heat to boiling, reduce heat and simmer 5 minutes uncovered. Stir gelatin into 1 cup cranberry juice to soften. Stir gelatin into hot cranberry mixture. Add remaining cranberry juice and Kirsch. Refrigerate until slightly thickened. Fold whipped cream into slightly thickened gelatin mixture. Pour mixture into 2-quart mold. Chill until firm. Make Raspberry Sauce. When ready to serve, dip mold into lukewarm water for a few seconds, tap to loosen and invert onto a serving platter. Garnish plate if desired. Serve each portion of Mousse with a little Raspberry Sauce. Serves 10.

Raspberry Sauce:
1 10-ounce package frozen raspberries
1 12-ounce jar raspberry preserves
¼ cup Kirsch or light rum

Press raspberries and juice through a sieve and discard seeds. Stir in preserves and Kirsch; mix well. Refrigerate covered.

Mrs. William D. Lyon (Marjorie)
Iosco County (East Tawas)

SOUTHERN COBBLER

1 stick butter
1 cup flour
1 cup sugar
3 teaspoons baking powder
¼ teaspoon salt
3 cups peaches, sliced
1 cup sugar

Melt butter in casserole dish. Mix flour, sugar, baking powder, salt and pour on butter. Do not mix and do not stir. Add the peaches and sugar. Do not mix and do not stir. Bake at 325 degrees for 1 hour. *Note: Serve with ice cream, whipped cream, or milk. Delicious, hot or cold.*

Elly M. Peterson
Eaton County (Charlotte)

CONCORD GRAPE PIE

3½ cups Concord grapes
1 cup sugar
¼ cup flour
¼ teaspoon salt
1 tablespoon lemon juice
   (fresh, frozen or canned)

1½ tablespoons butter or
   margarine, melted
1 9-inch unbaked pie shell

Slip skins from grapes and set skins aside. Bring pulp to boiling point and press through sieve to remove seeds. Add skins. Combine sugar, flour and salt. Add lemon juice, butter and grape pulp. Pour into unbaked shell. Sprinkle Crumb Topping over and bake at 400 degrees for 40 to 50 minutes.

Crumb Topping:
¾ cup flour
½ cup sugar

⅓ cup butter or margarine

Sift together flour and sugar. Cut in butter or margarine until crumbly. Sprinkle over pie before baking.

Ordella Kerckhoff
Oakland County (Farmington)

CHRISTMAS ANGEL CAKE

2 10-ounce packages frozen
   strawberries, thawed
   (reserve juice)
1 3-ounce package strawberry
   Jello

1 cup hot water
1 large Angel Food cake
1 carton whipped cream

Drain thawed strawberries, reserving the syrup (about 1 to 1¼ cups). Dissolve Jello in hot water, then stir in reserved syrup and refrigerate until slightly thickened, about 1 hour. Fold in drained berries to Jello mixture. Refrigerate until almost set, about 2 hours, stirring occasionally. Cut cake into 3 layers, spread the mixture on each layer and then frost with whipped cream.

Delores White
Branch County (Coldwater)

Fruit Basket

PINK CLOUD CAKE

1 package white cake mix
1 3-ounce package strawberry-flavored gelatin
1 cup boiling water
½ cup cold water
1 1-pound package frozen strawberry halves, thawed with ½ cup syrup reserved
1 3½-ounce package strawberry-whipped dessert mix
1 2 or 2⅛-ounce package dessert topping mix (Dream Whip)

Prepare cake according to package directions. Bake in two 9x1½-inch layer cake pans. Dissolve gelatin in boiling water; stir in cold water and set aside for 20 minutes. Cool cake 5 minutes in pans. Remove; place on racks over waxed paper. Using long-tined fork, punch holes in cake, making even rows across cake surface. Spoon gelatin over cake; chill 1 to 2 hours. Drain strawberries, reserving ½ cup syrup. Prepare strawberry whipped dessert mix according to package directions using berry syrup for the ½ cup water. Fold in berries. Spread 1 cup strawberry whipped dessert mix between layers; frost entire cake. Chill 1 hour. Prepare dessert topping mix according to package directions; spread over pink layer. *Note: You may substitute one 13x9x2-inch pan for the two 9x1½-inch layer cake pans. If you do so, leave cake in pan when frosting.*

Mrs. David Wolfe (Vickie)
Kalkaska County (Kalkaska)

. . . Stirring 1 pound of sugar into fruit after it is cooked and still warm, will make the fruit as sweet as 2¼ pounds of sugar added while fruit is boiling.

This special section was made possible by a gift from Whirlpool Corporation. The microwave oven recipes included herein are from the Whirlpool test kitchens.

Microwave

Microwave

TEMPERATURE SETTING CHART

NOTE: Microwave temperature settings vary from brand to brand. The recipes given in this cookbook were prepared and tested in Whirlpool microwave ovens. To adjust the timings of these recipes for use in your brand microwave oven, the following chart of equivalents, based on power wattage, should be helpful.

HIGH	= 100% of full power	= 650 watts
MED HI	= 73% of full power	= 475 watts
MED	= 50% of full power	= 325 watts
MED LO	= 30% of full power	= 200 watts
LO	= 15% of full power	= 100 watts

CRAB SPREAD

1 cup crabmeat, fresh, frozen or pasteurized
1 8-ounce package cream cheese, softened
1 tablespoon milk
2 teaspoon Worcestershire sauce
1 teaspoon onion juice
2 tablespoons slivered almonds, toasted
Assorted crackers

Thaw crabmeat if frozen. Remove any remaining pieces of shell or cartilage. In mixing bowl, combine cream cheese, milk, Worcestershire sauce and onion juice. Add crabmeat and blend well. Turn mixture into an 8-inch pie plate. Top with toasted almonds. Cook in microwave oven on HIGH approximately 2 minutes or until hot enough to serve. Serve warm with crackers. Makes about 2 cups.

BEEF TERIYAKI

1 pound boneless beef tenderloin or sirloin steak, cut 1-inch thick
4 cloves garlic, minced
½ cup soy sauce
¼ cup dry sherry
2 tablespoons sugar
2 teaspoons dry mustard

Thinly slice beef across the grain in bite-size strips. Combine garlic, soy sauce, sherry, sugar and mustard for marinade. Add steak to marinade and let stand for 2 to 3 hours at room temperature. Drain meat reserving marinade for basting. Thread meat strips accordion-style on small bamboo skewers and place in an 8½x12-inch baking dish. Cook skewers at HIGH for 4 to 5 minutes or until meat is done, brushing with reserved marinade and rearranging skewers twice.

SAUCY SAUCES FOR VEGETABLES

White Sauce:
2 tablespoons butter or
　margarine
2 tablespoons flour
¼ to ½ teaspoon salt
Dash of pepper
1 cup milk

In a 4-cup glass measure or a 1-quart casserole, melt butter or margarine for 30 to 45 seconds on HIGH. Blend in flour and seasonings until a smooth paste. Gradually add milk, stirring with a wire whisk until very smooth. Cook, uncovered for 3 to 4 minutes on HIGH until sauce boils and thickens, stirring at least halfway through. Serve warm. Yield: 1 cup. *Note: All of these sauces are good accompaniments to most vegetables, particularly cauliflower, broccoli, asparagus or Brussels sprouts.*

Variations:
Cheese Sauce:
Stir 1 cup shredded Cheddar cheese, ¼ teaspoon dry mustard and a dash of cayenne pepper into hot white sauce until cheese melts.

Mornay Sauce:
Add ½ cup shredded Swiss, gruyère or Parmesan cheese, 1 teaspoon lemon juice and a dash of cayenne to hot white sauce.

Curry Sauce:
Add 2 to 3 teaspoons curry powder with flour and seasonings. Nice served over cooked chicken as well as vegetables.

Béchamel Sauce:
Substitute ½ cup chicken stock plus ½ cup light cream (10%) for milk. Season with 1 teaspoon grated onion, dash pepper and thyme.

Dill Sauce:
Stir 2 teaspoons dill weed and 1 teaspoon lemon juice into hot white sauce. Serve with fish and vegetables.

. . . Microwave is an excellent "melter" for butter, cheese and chocolate chips.

Microwave

FESTIVE BROCCOLI CASSEROLE

½ cup onion, chopped
½ cup celery, chopped
¼ cup green pepper, chopped
2 tablespoons butter
1 10-ounce package chopped broccoli
1 can cream of mushroom soup
1 cup rice, cooked
½ cup Cheese Whiz
½ cup Cheddar cheese, grated or
½ can french fried onion rings

In a 1½-quart casserole, combine celery, onion, green pepper and butter. Microwave for 3 minutes at HIGH. Add broccoli and microwave 5 minutes at HIGH, stirring once during cooking. Add rice, soup and Cheese Whiz. Microwave 8 minutes at HIGH. Garnish with Cheddar cheese or onion rings. Microwave 1 minute at HIGH or until cheese melts or onion rings are heated through.

EASY HOT SEA DIP

4 5-ounce jars Old English Cheese Spread
2 7-ounce cans minced clams, drained
½ cup green pepper, diced
½ cup scallions, chopped
¼ teaspoon hot pepper sauce
¼ teaspoon garlic powder

Combine ingredients and microwave at MED HI for 6 to 8 minutes or until cheese is melted. Mix and serve hot with crackers or corn chips.

POTATOES AU GRATIN

4 cups potatoes, thinly sliced
½ cup butter or margarine
2 tablespoons flour
½ teaspoon seasoned salt
1 cup milk
⅛ teaspoon pepper
⅛ teaspoon celery seed
1 cup Cheddar cheese, grated
1 onion, thinly sliced
¼ cup Parmesan cheese, grated
Paprika

Arrange half of the sliced potatoes in a microwave ring mold or 1½-quart glass casserole. Melt butter or margarine in a 2-cup glass measure for 45 seconds to 1 minute on HIGH. Stir in flour and seasonings until a smooth paste. Gradually add milk until smooth and cook 3 to 4 minutes on HIGH until mixture thickens, stirring at least halfway through. Stir in Cheddar cheese and pour half of this mixture over the potatoes. Sprinkle with Parmesan cheese and paprika. Cover (1½-quart casserole lid fits ring mold nicely) and cook for 11 to 14 minutes on HIGH or until potatoes are tender. Let stand covered, 10 minutes before serving. Serves 4 to 5.

ARTICHOKES WITH YOGURT HERB DIP

2 artichokes, about ¾ pound each
1 clove, garlic, minced
1 tablespoon fresh lemon juice

Wash artichokes under cold water; drain. Cut off stem ends and about 1 inch of tops. Snip off prickly tip of each leaf with kitchen scissors. Combine ½ cup water, lemon juice and garlic in 3-quart glass casserole. Add artichokes; cover and cook on HIGH for 12 to 15 minutes, or until stem end is fork tender. Let stand, covered, 10 minutes.

Yogurt Herb Dip:
¼ cup cucumber, finely chopped
1 cup low-fat plain yogurt
½ teaspoon dill weed
¼ teaspoon salt
¼ teaspoon garlic powder
Paprika

Combine all ingredients except paprika. Mix well. Dust with paprika and serve chilled with artichokes.

CHICKEN KIEV

6 chicken breasts, skinned and boned
¼ cup butter or margarine, softened
1 tablespoon parsley, finely minced
1 clove garlic, finely minced
¼ cup flour
1 egg
⅓ cup bread crumbs
½ teaspoon salt
Dash of pepper
¼ cup butter or margarine, melted

Stir parsley and garlic into softened butter or margarine. Shape into a stick and chill or freeze until firm. Meanwhile place chicken breast between 2 pieces of waxed paper and pound it until quite thin. Be careful not to tear chicken. Slice chilled butter or margarine into 6 pieces. Place 1 square into each chicken breast and roll, jellyroll fashion to completely enclose butter. Secure with toothpicks. Dip rolls into flour, then egg beaten with 1 tablespoon water and then into crumbs seasoned with salt and pepper. Chill 1 hour. Roll chicken rolls in melted butter and arrange on a microwave roasting rack and dish. Cover with waxed paper and cook 9 to 11 minutes on HIGH, turning over halfway through, until chicken is tender. Let stand 5 to 10 minutes before serving. Serves 6.

Microwave

STUFFED EGGPLANT

1 medium eggplant
1 small onion, chopped
1 tomato, peeled and chopped
2 cloves garlic, minced
½ teaspoon dried parsley

Salt and pepper to taste
1 cup chicken or ham, diced and cooked
1 tablespoon Parmesan cheese

Wash and pierce eggplant. Cut eggplant in half lengthwise. Arrange halves on microwave roasting rack and dish. Cover and cook 6 to 7 minutes on HIGH until flesh is very tender, rearranging halfway through cooking cycle. Scoop out flesh, being careful not to damage the skin. Chop flesh and combine with onion, tomato, garlic and seasonings. Add chicken or ham and fill eggplant shells. Sprinkle with grated Parmesan cheese. Arrange filled halves on same rack and dish. Cover and cook for 2 to 3 minutes on HIGH or until filling is hot and cheese has melted. Let stand, covered, 5 to 10 minutes before serving. Serves 3 to 4.

BROCCOLI BEEF

1 bunch fresh broccoli
1 flank steak, sliced diagonally in ¼-inch strips
1 tablespoon cornstarch

1 tablespoon soy sauce
1 clove garlic, finely minced
¼ teaspoon salt
2 tablespoons cooking oil

Cut broccoli into small flowerettes 1½ inches long and with stalks about ¼ inch in diameter. Place flowerettes in a baking dish with stalks on the outer edge of the dish and buds in the middle. Cover loosely with plastic wrap and microwave on HIGH for 6 to 8 minutes or until tender crisp. Preheat browning dish for 6 minutes on HIGH with cover on dish. Combine meat strips with cornstarch, soy sauce, garlic, salt, pepper, and cooking oil. Toss the meat mixture into the browning dish, stirring to sear meat. Cover and microwave on HIGH for 3 minutes, stirring twice. Add gravy. Do not cover. Microwave for 3 minutes on HIGH stirring twice. It is not necessary to remove browning dish from oven when adding meat or gravy. Toss in the cooked broccoli to meat and gravy mixture. Serve with rice.

SHISH KABOB

½ cup wine vinegar
½ cup cooking oil
1 teaspoon onion salt
1 clove garlic, split in half
¼ cup soy sauce
½ cup water
2 teaspoons Italian seasoning
2 pounds boneless sirloin steak, cut in 1-inch cubes
½ pound small fresh mushrooms
1 dozen tomato wedges
1 green pepper, seeded and cut in 1-inch squares
2 cups precooked white rice

Combine vinegar, oil, onion salt, garlic, soy sauce, water and Italian seasoning in a large mixing bowl. Add steak cubes to marinade and let stand at room temperature for 3 to 4 hours. Wash mushrooms, quarter tomatoes and cut green pepper. Drain meat, reserving marinade for basting. Place meat cubes and desired vegetables alternating on long wooden skewers. Place 3 skewers in a 6x11-inch baking dish, baste with marinade. Cook uncovered for 4 minutes on HIGH for medium rare meat. Turn skewers over once and baste with marinade during cooking period. Cook slightly longer for well done meat. Repeat with remaining shish kabobs. Serve on bed of white rice.

. . . Thaw frozen vegetables in their package with a microwave.

STUFFED CABBAGE ROLLS

8 large cabbage leaves
1 pound lean ground beef
1 cup rice, cooked
1 egg
1 teaspoon instant minced onion
½ teaspoon sage
1½ cups commercially prepared spaghetti sauce

To remove leaves from cabbage, rinse head with water and loosely wrap in waxed paper. Microwave on HIGH for 2 to 3 minutes or until outer leaves peel off easily. With a sharp knife, cut out hard cores from softened leaves. Combine ground beef, rice, egg, onion and sage and mix thoroughly. Form into 8 small loaves. Place a loaf in center of each cabbage leaf. Fold sides of leaf over filling and roll up ends to form meat package. Arrange cabbage rolls, seam side down in an 8½x12-inch baking dish. Spoon on spaghetti sauce. Cover with waxed paper. Microwave 3 minutes on HIGH. Reduce setting to MED and microwave 12 minutes.

Microwave

ROAST "PIG" HAWAIIAN

Pork loin roast (4 to 5 pounds or less)
Hickory flavored liquid smoke
1 cup coarse salt (Kosher or pretzel salt)
Large brown paper bag
Ti leaves (optional, if available)

Generously brush roast with liquid smoke. For a stronger smoke flavor, pierce roast with a fork, brush generously with liquid smoke, seal tightly in a plastic bag and refrigerate overnight. Roll roast in the salt until completely covered (it may look like too much salt, but it won't be). Wrap roast in ti leaves if available. Place roast in brown paper bag and wrap it around roast tightly. Place in a 2-quart flat glass baking dish. Microwave 10 to 11 minutes per pound on MED. Allow to stand 10 to 15 minutes, then microwave an additional 5 minutes per pound.

LONDON BROIL LORD ESSEX

1 2-pound flank steak
1 tablespoon bottled gravy concentrate
1 tablespoon vegetable oil
1 teaspoon lemon juice
1 clove garlic, minced
2 teaspoons chopped parsley
Salt
Pepper

Place steak in marinade (see below), turning several times to coat meat. Let stand at room temperature for 2 to 4 hours, turn over several times. Combine gravy concentrate, oil, lemon juice, garlic and parsley. To cook steak, remove from marinade and place on a meat rack in a 8½x12-inch baking dish. Spread with gravy mixture. Microwave for about 12 to 14 minutes on HIGH for medium rare meat. Remove steak from oven and let stand covered with aluminim foil for 15 minutes. Salt and pepper to taste. Slice very thinly on diagonal across the grain.

Lemon Marinade:
½ cup lemon juice
½ cup salad oil
1 tablespoon chopped parsley
2 bay leaves
1 clove garlic, crushed
2 slices onion
1 tablespoon sugar
Pinch of nutmeg
2 drops hot pepper sauce

Combine ingredients for marinade and mix well.

CRYSTALLIZED ORANGE NUTS

¼ cup orange juice
1 cup sugar

2 cups pecan halves

Combine sugar and orange juice in a 2-quart 12x7-inch glass baking dish and mix well. Stir in pecans. Microwave for 6 minutes at MED HI. Stir and continue cooking for 8 minutes, or until syrup crystallizes. Spread, separate and cool glazed nuts on buttered cookie sheet.

PEANUT CHO-CO NUT FUDGE

1 12-ounce package chocolate chips
½ cup chunky peanut butter
1 14-ounce can sweetened condensed milk

½ cup coconut
½ cup walnuts, chopped

Melt chocolate chips at MED HI for 2½ minutes. Stir until melted. Add peanut butter and condensed milk and blend. Cook at MED HI for 1½ minutes. Add coconut and nuts. Pour into an 8½x12-inch dish. Cool before cutting.

POPCORN WREATH

Wreath:
8 cups popped corn
1 cup M & M's candy
1 cup Spanish peanuts

1 cup colored miniature marshmallows

Measure popcorn into a large bowl. Pour syrup in a thin stream over popcorn stirring until all kernels are well coated. Add M & M's, peanuts and marshmallows. Mix well. Pack into a well-greased ring mold. Cool and unmold on serving plate.

Syrup:
¾ cup granulated sugar
¾ cup brown sugar
½ cup light corn syrup
½ cup water

1 teaspoon white vinegar
¼ teaspoon salt
¾ cup butter

In an 8-cup measure, combine all ingredients for the syrup except butter. Microwave on HIGH for 12 to 13 minutes, stirring every 3 minutes. Cook until small amount of mixture dropped into cold water forms a hard ball, or 260 degrees with a candy thermometer. Add butter and mix well.

Microwave

PEANUT BRITTLE

1 cup raw peanuts
1 cup sugar
½ cup white corn syrup
⅛ teaspoon salt

1 teaspoon baking soda
1 teaspoon vanilla
1 teaspoon butter

In a 1½-quart casserole, stir together peanuts, sugar, syrup and salt. Cook on HIGH for 8 minutes, stirring well after 4 minutes. Add butter and vanilla. Cook on HIGH for 1 minute longer. Add baking soda and quickly stir until light and foamy. Immediately pour onto lightly buttered baking sheet. Spread out thin. When cool, break into pieces.

QUICK PEACH CRUMBLE

½ cup butter or margarine
1 2-layer size package butter brickle cake mix
1 3½-ounce can flaked coconut

1 teaspoon ground cinnamon
1 29-ounce can sliced peaches, drained
Vanilla ice cream

In 12x7½x2-inch baking dish, melt butter at HIGH for about 1 minute 15 seconds. Stir in dry cake mix, coconut and cinnamon; mix well. Remove 1⅓ cups of the mixture; press remaining into dish. Cook, uncovered, at HIGH for 5 minutes, giving dish half turn once. Top with peach slices. Crumble remaining coconut mixture over top. Cook, uncovered, at HIGH for 12 minutes, giving dish half turn once. Serve warm or cool topped with ice cream. Serves 10 to 12.

APPLE MAPLE PUDDING

4 to 5 medium apples, pared and thinly sliced
¾ cup maple syrup
2 eggs
¼ cup brown sugar

1 tablespoon butter or margarine, melted
1 cup all-purpose flour
1 teaspoon salt
½ teaspoon baking powder

Place sliced apples in microwave ring mold. Cover with maple syrup. Cook for 1 minute on HIGH. Beat together eggs, brown sugar and melted margarine. Stir into apples until blended. Combine remaining ingredients and stir thoroughly into apple mixture until completely moistened. Bake 3 to 4 minutes on HIGH until almost set. Let stand 5 to 10 minutes to cool and completely set. Serves 4 to 5.

This special section was compiled for the *Michigan Cooks' Collection* by Fred Graczyk, former proprietor of The Vineyards Restaurant in Southfield, Michigan.

Michigan Restaurant Sampler

Restaurant Sampler

PORK ROAST WITH SWEET AND SOUR SAUCE
The Vineyards, Southfield, Michigan

From your favorite butcher, purchase four 1 pound center cut rib (not loin) pork roasts. Place in roasting pan bone-side down and brown in oven at 450 degrees for 30 minutes. Remove from oven when well browned and transfer to deeper baking dish. Pour Sweet and Sour Sauce over pork and bake for 2½ hours at 300 degrees, or until pork is tender. Baste occasionally. Serve on platter with sauce ladled over pork. Garnish with baked apple. Serves 4 generously.

Sweet and Sour Sauce:

2 cups sugar
1 cup distilled vinegar
2 tablespoons green pepper, chopped
1 teaspoon salt

1 cup water
4 teaspoons cornstarch mixed with 2 tablespoons cold water
2 teaspoons paprika
Parsley, finely chopped

Mix sugar, vinegar, green pepper and salt with 1 cup water. Simmer 5 minutes. Combine cornstarch and 2 tablespoons cold water, add to mixture. Cook and stir until sauce thickens. Let cool. Before serving, strain out vegetables. Add paprika and a bit of finely chopped parsley. Makes about 2 cups.

VEAL SCALLOPINE
Franky's Restaurant, Niles, Michigan

12 2-ounce pieces veal cutlet
½ cup flour
3 tablespoons butter
8 slices onion
8 thick tomato slices
8 large pieces green pepper, cooked

4 cups beef bouillon
2 cups mushrooms, sliced and cooked
6 ounces dry sherry
Salt, pepper, oregano and garlic powder to taste

Flatten veal medallions very thin. Dredge in flour and brown in butter. Remove veal. In the same pan, sauté onion, tomato slices and green pepper. Add bouillon. Let simmer. Add mushrooms, sherry and seasonings. Simmer for about 5 minutes. Put meat on plates and cover with sauce. Serves 4.

THE EMBERS' PORK CHOPS
The Embers, Mt. Pleasant, Michigan

Marinade:
6 1-pound pork chops
2 cups soy sauce
1 cup water
½ cup brown sugar
1 tablespoon dark molasses
1 teaspoon salt

Mix soy sauce, water, brown sugar, molasses and salt. Bring to a boil and let cool. Put chops in a pan with bone-side up. Pour the sauce over the pork chops and let stand overnight in refrigerator. Next day take pork chops out of sauce and place in baking pan. Cover tightly with foil. Bake at 375 degrees about 2 hours (until tender). While chops are baking, combine all Red Sauce ingredients in heavy saucepan or double boiler.

Red Sauce:
⅓ cup water
1 14-ounce bottle Heinz Ketchup
1 12-ounce bottle Heinz Chili Sauce
½ cup brown sugar
1 tablespoon dry mustard

Dilute dry mustard, sugar and water together leaving no lumps. Bring all ingredients to a slight boil. The Red Sauce is finished. After chops are tender, remove from oven and dip in the Red Sauce. Take chops after dipping and place in baking pan and bake for 30 minutes at 350 degrees until slightly glazed. *Note: Marinating sauce and Red Sauce may be reused if brought to a boil and stored in refrigerator or frozen. For an extra flavor, keep at room temperature until you are ready to put on charcoal pit or grill. Have grill as high as possible from coals, a large bed of coals is not needed. Place finished chops on grill, let cook slowly, a little blacking does not hurt the chops–grilling should not take more than 15 minutes.*

Restaurant Sampler

PRIME LONDON BROIL
Haab's Restaurant, Ypsilanti, Michigan

Marinade:
1 cup red wine
⅓ cup vinegar
½ cup salad oil
¼ teaspoon sweet basil
¼ teaspoon oregano
¼ teaspoon black pepper

2 teaspoons salt
1¼ teaspoons Accent
1 small clove fresh garlic, crushed
2 tablespoons onion, chopped
1 bay leaf, broken

Combine all ingredients for marinade. Immerse steaks in marinade, cover and let stand for 8 hours under refrigeration.

Steaks:
6 10-ounce boneless Prime
Top 1-inch thick sirloin steaks

Broil steaks to preferred degree of doneness. Yield: 6 servings.

TOSI'S BISTECCA AL PEPE NERO
Tosi's, Stevensville, Michigan

1 1 to 1¼-inch thick club steak
2 tablespoons pepper pods, crushed
1 tablespoon cooking oil

½ cup Burgundy wine
½ cup *Au Jus*
1 tablespoon butter

Coarsely crush peppers with side of a cleaver or a hammer. Press crushed pepper pods into both sides of the steak. On *charcoal or broiler,* sear both sides of the steak. In a large skillet, prepare wine, *Au Jus* and butter. Allow sauce to simmer. Remove steak from broiler or charcoal, and place in sauce. Heat at 375 degrees. Remove steak from skillet and place on hot platter, when desired doneness is reached. Sauce should be poured over steak.

ARNI KAPAMA
Jim's Tiffany Place, Lansing, Michigan

8 lamb shanks (approximately 10 ounces)
Salt, pepper and 2 tablespoons leaf oregano
1 cup onions, finely chopped
1 garlic clove, crushed
6 large tomatoes, peeled and crushed
1 10¾-ounce can condensed tomato soup
4 ounces dark cooking sherry
1 cinnamon stick

Season lamb with salt, pepper and oregano on baking sheet pan. Bake for 45 minutes at 400 degrees. Prepare sauce while lamb is in oven. Sauté onions and garlic in olive oil until lightly browned. Combine crushed tomatoes, soup, sherry and cinnamon stick. Add to onion mixture; simmer on low heat for 30 minutes. Remove lamb from oven and place in roasting pot. Scrape all drippings from sheet pan into kapama sauce. Pour sauce over lamb. Cover and bake for 2 hours at 375 degrees. Lamb is tender when meat begins to separate from bone. Allow sauce to rest for 15 minutes, skim fat. Ladle sauce over lamb and serve with rice.

CHICKEN DELMAR
Grand Hotel, Mackinac Island, Michigan

3½ pound chicken, leg and thigh only
Melted butter
Cracker crumbs

Roll leg and thigh in melted butter and then in cracker crumbs. Place on large drip pan and bake at 450 degrees for 20 minutes. Reduce heat to 275 degrees and bake until very tender, about 1½ hours. Serve with a cream-like gravy made from chicken stock and thickened with flour and cream. Add small amount of sage and poultry seasoning.

Restaurant Sampler

CHICKEN GABRIELLE
Pontchartrain Wine Cellars, Detroit, Michigan

3 pounds chicken, cooked and diced
1 pound broccoli or asparagus spears, cooked
3 cups cream of mushroom soup
1 cup cream
1 teaspoon curry powder
4 drops Tabasco sauce
4 tablespoons pimento, chopped
4 tablespoons Parmesan cheese, grated
Paprika

Place broccoli or asparagus in greased shallow baking dish. Arrange chicken over. Combine soup, cream, curry powder and Tabasco. Heat, stirring constantly, until smooth. Add pimento. Pour sauce over chicken and sprinkle with cheese and paprika. Bake for 15 minutes at 400 degrees. Serves 8.

LE POULET AU VINAIGRE
Aliette's Bakery, Detroit, Michigan

1 large young chicken, cut in 4
Flour
¼ pound butter
4 cloves garlic, chopped fine
1 large onion, chopped fine
½ cup tarragon wine vinegar
½ cup dry white wine
1 tablespoon tomato paste
Beef or veal bouillon
1 tablespoon Dijon mustard

Flour and brown chicken in half the butter. Add the garlic, onion, vinegar, wine, tomato paste and enough bouillon to cover the chicken. Cook slowly. When done, remove chicken and keep hot. Remove fat from sauce. Add tomato paste if necessary. Remove sauce from stove and add remaining butter and the mustard, beating vigorously until incorporated into the sauce. Dress chicken on serving dish and strain the sauce over it. Serve very hot. Serves 4.

TERIYAKI CHICKEN
Hilton Shanty Creek, Bellaire, Michigan

Marinate boneless chicken breasts in equal parts of sherry, soy sauce and pineapple juice for 2 hours. Broil until done, about 5 minutes, turning once. Serve on wild rice topped with sauce.

Sauce:
Heat equal parts of brown sugar and butter, then add water to prevent brown sugar from sticking. Bring to a simmer but do not boil. Add dissolved cornstarch and water to achieve desired thickness. Let simmer 3 or 4 minutes. Pour over chicken and rice. Top with pineapple slices.

PEANUT CHICKEN
Ah Wok Restaurant, Novi, Michigan

2 to 3 chicken breasts
¼ cup cornstarch
6 egg whites
4 tablespoons vegetable oil, divided
2 cups vegetable oil

¼ cup diced bamboo shoots
¼ cup sliced water chestnuts
¼ cup green peas
½ cup fresh roasted peanuts
¼ cup chicken broth

Cut chicken breasts into 1-inch slices. Marinate for 1 hour in cornstarch, egg whites and 1 tablespoon of vegetable oil. Heat 2 cups of oil in a wok or large saucepan. Cook chicken for 3 minutes in hot oil, strain and set aside. Into another saucepan add 3 tablespoons of vegetable oil and heat over hot flame. Add bamboo shoots, water chestnuts, green peas and peanuts. Stir fry for 2 minutes. Add chicken meat to saucepan and chicken broth. Bring to full quick boil.

Add: ½ teaspoon sugar
½ teaspoon sesame oil
½ teaspoon Accent
Salt to taste

Tabasco sauce and hot pepper powder to taste

Thicken whole mixture with a cornstarch solution of 4 tablespoons of cornstarch to ½ cup water. Serve over boiled rice. Serves 2 to 3.

CHEESE SOUFFLÉ
Gibbs Country House, Ludington, Michigan

6 eggs
4 cups milk
½ teaspoon dry mustard
½ pound sharp Cheddar cheese, grated

1 loaf buttered bread, diced into ½-inch cubes
Melted margarine
Seasoning salt

Mix eggs, milk, mustard and salt. In a 10x13-inch pan layer bread cubes and grated cheese making 3 layers. Saturate with milk mixture (top layer should be cheese). Let sit overnight. Bake for 1 hour at 350 degrees.

SHRIMP AND CRAB STUFFED FLOUNDER
Shalea Inn, Auburn Heights, Michigan

4 1½-pound flounders, cleaned with heads removed, but tails intact
1½ pounds shrimp, uncooked
10 tablespoons butter, cut into ½-inch bits, plus 3 tablespoons butter, melted
1½ cups soft fresh crumbs, made from French or Italian-type white bread, pulverized in a blender
⅓ cup onions, finely chopped
⅓ cup green peppers, finely chopped
⅓ cup celery, finely chopped
⅓ cup scallions, finely chopped, including 3 inches of the green
⅓ cup canned tomatoes, drained and finely chopped
4 teaspoons Worcestershire sauce
1½ teaspoons Creole Mustard
½ teaspoon ground hot red pepper
2 teaspoons salt
1 pound (2 cups) fresh, frozen or canned crabmeat, thoroughly drained and picked over to remove all bits of shell or cartilage
3 tablespoons fresh parsley, finely chopped (preferably the flat-leaf Italian variety)
¼ teaspoon freshly ground black pepper

In a heavy 10 to 12-inch skillet, melt 6 tablespoons of the butter bits over moderate heat. When the foam begins to subside, add the bread crumbs and stir until they are crisp and golden. With rubber spatula, scrape the entire contents of the skillet into a deep bowl and set aside. Add the remaining 4 tablespoons of butter bits to the skillet and melt them over moderate heat. Drop in the onions, green peppers, celery, scallions, and garlic and, stirring frequently, cook for about 5 minutes, or until the vegetables are soft, but not brown. Stir in the tomatoes, Worcestershire sauce, Creole mustard, red pepper and 1 teaspoon salt. Then scrape the mixture into the bowl with the bread crumbs. Add the reserved shrimp, the crabmeat and the parsley, and toss all the stuffing ingredients together gently but thoroughly. Taste for seasoning. Preheat the oven to 400 degrees. With a pastry brush, spread 1 tablespoon of the melted butter over the bottom and sides of a shallow baking-serving dish large enough to hold the flounders in one layer. Set aside. Wash the fish under cold running water and pat them dry with paper towels. To prepare the flounders for stuffing, place one at a time on its belly (light-colored side) on the cutting board. With a small sharp knife, make a 4 to 5-inch long slit completely through the skin and top surface of flesh to the backbone of the fish, cutting from about 1 inch behind the head to within about 1 inch of the tail. With your fingers on the point of the knife, gently lift the top surface of the flesh away from the rows of small bones radiating from the backbone, to create pockets on both sides of the slit. Sprinkle the remaining teaspoon of the salt and the

(Recipe continued on next page)

black pepper inside the pockets formed in the flounder. Then fill the pockets and the space between them with the shrimp-and-crab stuffing, dividing it equally among the 4 fish and mounding the stuffing in the centers. Arrange the flounders side by side in the buttered dish and brush the tops with the remaining 2 tablespoons of melted butter. Bake on the middle shelf of the oven for about 20 minutes or until the fish feel firm when prodded gently with a finger. Serve the shrimp-and-crab-stuffed flounder at once, directly from the baking dish. Serves 4.

STUFFED RED SNAPPER WITH SHRIMP
Lakewood Inn, Battle Creek, Michigan

4 pieces 8 to 10-ounce Red Snapper filets
1 cup shrimp, diced
⅓ cup celery, diced
¼ cup green peppers, diced
1 teaspoon onion, diced
⅓ cup mushrooms, diced
1 cup butter, divided
2 cups cracker crumbs

¼ teaspoon seasoning salt
¼ teaspoon garlic granules
½ teaspoon lemon juice
½ cup Sauterne wine
Pinch of salt, pepper, and Accent
Dash of Tabasco and Worcestershire sauce
Dash of paprika

Sauté diced shrimp, celery, green peppers, onion and mushrooms in ½ cup butter very slightly. Add the remaining ingredients and mix well. Place mixture on Red Snapper filets and sprinkle on a little paprika. Bake at 350 degrees for 15 minutes.

INN'S BROOK TROUT
Bay Valley Inn, Bay City, Michigan

Use a whole boned brook trout per portion. Lightly salt inside cavity and lightly flour outside. In hot oil, sauté each side, 6 minutes per side. Remove from oil and keep warm. In 1½ ounces clarified butter, sauté together:

¼ peeled, seeded and sliced cucumber
4 button mushrooms, thickly sliced

3 medium size shrimp, cooked, peeled and deveined
½ ounce white Sauterne wine
Juice of ¼ lemon

Sauté for 5 minutes and serve over trout.

Restaurant Sampler

SCALLOPED OYSTERS AND CORN
Fogcutter Restaurant, Port Huron, Michigan

1 pint small stewing oysters, reserve juice
1 medium can whole kernel corn, drained
1 cup crushed crackers, rolled fine
½ cup butter or margarine, melted
1 teaspoon onion, finely chopped
Shake of nutmeg
Shake of paprika
Salt and pepper
1 cup milk

Grease shallow baking pan. Put oysters and juice on bottom of pan and sprinkle with ½ of cracker crumbs. Sprinkle with onion. Pour over ½ of melted butter, then cover with can of corn, then rest of oysters and juice, remainder of crumbs and butter. Shake nutmeg, paprika, salt and pepper on top. Cover with milk. Bake at 350 degrees for 45 minutes to 1 hour (until not soupy). Yield: 8 servings.

CHICKEN MULLIGATAWNEY SOUP
Hathaway House Restaurant, Blissfield, Michigan

2 quarts chicken stock
¾ pound canned tomatoes, chopped
½ cup rice
2 cloves
4 ounces celery, chopped
4 ounces green apples, chopped
4 ounces, onions, chopped
4 ounces green peppers, chopped
2 ounces butter or margarine
¼ cup flour
1½ teaspoons curry powder
1½ teaspoons salt
¼ teaspoon ground pepper
1 pint milk (16 ounces)
4 ounces chicken, cooked

Bring chicken stock to a boil; add tomatoes, rice, cloves, celery, apples, onions and green peppers. Simmer 30 minutes. In separate pan, simmer butter and flour for 10 minutes, but don't allow to brown. To butter mixture add curry powder, salt, ground pepper and milk. Whip until smooth and add to soup. Dice the cooked chicken and add to soup. *Voila!! Bon Appetit!* Serves 12.

CHARLEY'S CHOWDER
Gandy Dancer, Ann Arbor, Michigan

2 ounces olive oil
3 medium garlic cloves, crushed
2 ounces onions, finely chopped
3 ounces celery, finely chopped
A pinch each of: oregano, basil and thyme
6 ounces stewed tomatoes, very finely chopped
3 pints water
3 pints clam juice or clamato juice
1 pound boneless fish, pollack or turbot
Salt to taste
1 ounce parsley, finely chopped

Place olive oil in large pot and heat on stove until very hot. Drop the crushed garlic cloves into the hot oil. Cook the cloves of garlic until *golden* in color. It is very important that you do not burn the garlic as this will ruin the taste. Remove the cloves from the oil. While the oil is hot, add the onions and cook for a minute or two. Add the basil, oregano and thyme and cook for another minute. Add the celery and cook until translucent in color. Add the finely chopped tomatoes and cook for about 20 to 25 mintues, stirring to prevent sticking. Add water, fish, clam juice and cook for an additional 15 minutes, uncovered at full heat. This removes moisture to purify and extract oils for flavoring the chowder. Add salt, cover the pot and keep cooking for another 20 minutes at low heat. Stir often by whipping to break up the fish and blend the flavor. When serving, add the chopped parsley. *Note: When serving this soup as an appetizer, use parsley as the recipe indicates. If using as the court bouillon for bouillabaisse, eliminate the chopped parsley.*

OLD FASHION CREAM OF TOMATO SOUP
Sinbads-St. Clair Inn, St. Clair, Michigan

1 gallon milk
2 No. 2½ cans whole tomatoes
Salt and pepper to taste
1 tablespoon baking soda

Heat milk to scalding point. Mash tomatoes and beat just until it comes to a boil. Add salt and pepper and soda to tomatoes. Pour tomatoes into scalded milk and stir. Serves 18 to 20. *Note: Tomatoes must be added to milk, not the milk to the tomatoes.*

JOE MUER'S BEAN RELISH
Joe Muer's, Detroit, Michigan

There are three very important rules about this relish that are commonly misunderstood. First, the beans must be started in cold water—no pre-soaking. Second, cook the beans slowly, adding water when necessary. Third, retain the water in which the beans are cooked. (There is no oil in this recipe.)

2 quarts Great Northern Beans
Salt and pepper to taste
1 cup minced parsley
1 cup onions, minced
Vinegar to taste

Start beans in cold water and cook at low heat, adding water as it boils down. Occasionally, turn beans with wooden spoon to allow even cooking. Cooking time is hard to judge, so test occasionally by pinching a bean. When *just* soft, they are done. When cool, add parsley and onion. Mix in vinegar. Add small amounts of vinegar at a time, tasting as you go. *Note: Cooked beans can be reserved in their own juice in the refrigerator without the seasonings and vinegar for future use.*

GERMAN POTATO SALAD
Northwoods Supper Club, Marquette, Michigan

6 ounces bacon, fried, crumbled and set aside (reserve drippings)
¾ cup onion, finely chopped
¾ cup celery, finely chopped
2 cups water
½ cup sugar
1½ teaspoons salt
2½ teaspoons flour
Dash pepper
½ teaspoon dry mustard
½ cup cider vinegar
1 to 1½ pounds potatoes, boiled in jackets

Fry the bacon and set aside. Sauté in bacon drippings the onion and celery. Add water while vegetables are still crisp and bring to a boil. Combine sugar, salt, flour, pepper and dry mustard. Stir dry ingredients into boiling mixture to thicken. Remove from heat and add vinegar. Boil potatoes in jackets, remove jackets and slice when done. Add crumbled bacon to celery and onion mixture and fold into sliced potatoes. Enjoy!! *Note: May be garnished with sliced hard-cooked egg.*

SQUASH BREAD
Mayflower Hotel, Plymouth, Michigan

Squash bread is seldom seen nowadays, but is well worth making. To 1 cup of sifted squash, add 2 tablespoonfuls of sugar, 1 teaspoonful of salt, 1½ cupfuls of scalded milk and 1 tablespoonful of butter. When cool, add ½ yeast cake and flour enough to knead 15 minutes. When risen, knead again, shape into loaves, and bake, when light.

FRENCH CHOCOLATE PIE
Point West, Holland, Michigan

4 9-inch pie shells	14 whole eggs
1½ pounds whipped butter	8 ounces Bakers chocolate, melted
2 pounds powdered sugar	2 tablespoons vanilla

Combine butter, sugar and vanilla and whip for 2 minutes with paddle on first speed. Scrape bowl and paddle, whip again for 2 minutes on second speed. Scrape and whip again for 2 minutes on third speed. Scrape bowl and paddle and add melted chocolate. Whip on second speed for 5 minutes. Scrape bowl and paddle and whip on third speed for 4 minutes. Take out paddle, scrape and replace with wire whip. Turn to third speed and add eggs one at a time always while whipping. When all eggs are in, stop machine, scrape bowl, and whip. Spoon into pie shells. Refrigerate for 6 hours before serving.

WINE PIE
Win Schuler's, Marshall, Michigan

2 9-inch graham cracker pie crusts	1 pound raisins, soaked in ½ cup water and ½ cup vermouth overnight
1 pound vanilla instant pudding mix	1 pint whipping cream
1 cup sweet vermouth	2½ ounces nuts, chopped
2½ cups milk	

Prepare vanilla pudding using vermouth and milk. Soak raisins overnight in ½ cup of water and ½ cup vermouth. Whip cream and fold into pudding with nuts and drained raisins. Pour filling into 2 prepared graham cracker shells. Freeze until firm. To serve, thaw slightly and decorate with whipped cream.

Restaurant Sampler

CHOCOLATE STRATA PIE
House of Ludington, Escanaba, Michigan

1 cup all-purpose flour, sifted
½ teaspoon salt
⅓ cup shortening
3 to 4 tablespoons cold water
2 egg whites

½ teaspoon vinegar
¼ teaspoon salt
¼ teaspoon cinnamon, if desired
½ cup sugar

Sift together flour and ½ teaspoon salt into mixing bowl. Cut in shortening until particles are the size of small peas. Sprinkle cold water over mixture while tossing and stirring lightly with fork. Add liquid to driest particles pushing lumps to side, until dough is just moist enough to hold together. Form into a ball. Flatten to ½-inch thickness; smooth edges. Roll out dough to a circle 1½ inches larger than an inverted 9-inch pie pan. Fit loosely into pan; gently pat out air pockets. Fold edge to form a standing rim; flute. Prick generously with a fork. Bake at 450 degrees for 10 to 12 minutes until golden brown. Beat 2 egg whites with vinegar, salt and cinnamon until soft mounds form. Add sugar gradually. Continue beating until meringue stands in stiff, glossy peaks. Spread bottom and sides of baked pie shell with meringue. Bake at 325 degrees for 15 to 18 minutes until lightly browned. Cool and fill. *Note: If you use self-rising flour, omit salt.*

Filling:
2 egg yolks, slightly beaten
¼ cup water
1 6-ounce package Nestles Semi-Sweet chocolate morsels

¼ cup sugar
¼ teaspoon cinnamon
1 cup whipping cream

Add slightly beaten egg yolks and water to melted Nestlé's Semi-Sweet chocolate morsels. Spread 3 tablespoons over cooled meringue. Chill remainder. Combine sugar, cinnamon and whipping cream. Beat until thick. Spread ½ the whipping cream over the chocolate in the pie shell. Combine the remaining whipped cream with the chocolate mixture that was reserved. Spread over whipped cream in pie shell. Chill at least 4 hours.

. . . Place hardened sugar in warm oven for 10 to 15 minutes to soften.

CHOCOLATE MOUSSE
Tweeny's Cafe, Birmingham, Michigan

8 ounces Tobler's bittersweet chocolate
1 cup superfine sugar
½ cup weak coffee
10 egg yolks
¼ cup liqueur
10 egg whites

Melt chocolate, superfine sugar and weak coffee. Melt and blend over double boiler. Remove from heat and leave in double boiler. Beat in 10 egg yolks, one at a time. Remove from top of double boiler and cool. Stir in ¼ cup liqueur flavoring and fold in 10 beaten egg whites. Cover with Saran Wrap and chill 24 hours before serving. Serves 10.

APPLE CLAFOUTE
Golden Mushroom Restaurant, Detroit, Michigan

Batter:
1 pint milk
6 ounces sugar
¼ teaspoon salt
Few drops vanilla
6 ounces flour, sifted
6 eggs
2 tablespoons clarified butter
Powdered sugar

Mix together milk, sugar, salt, vanilla and flour until smooth. Add eggs to batter and whip or blend smooth. Preheat a 10x15x1½-inch cakepan in 375 degree oven. Pour in the clarified butter and spread over bottom. Pour in just enough batter to cover the bottom of the pan (about ⅛ inch deep). Place in oven to set. Spread the apples evenly over the bottom and pour rest of batter in. Bake at 375 degrees for about 50 minutes or until done. Serve warm with sprinkled sugar. Serves 12.

Apples:
4 pounds Northern Spy or Jonathan apples, peeled, cored and sliced ⅜ inch thick
½ cup butter, melted
1 lemon rind, grated
½ teaspoon cinnamon
½ cup applejack (or brandy or rum)
4 ounces brown sugar

Heat a large skillet and add apples and butter. Cook over high heat, turning apples carefully until they are tender, but not mushy. Spread them to cool. When cold, add lemon rind, cinnamon, applejack and brown sugar. Spread the apples evenly over the set batter.

POACHED PEARS WITH GRAND MARNIER ZABAGLIONE
London Chop House, Detroit, Michigan

2 quarts water
2 pounds sugar
Juice of 1 lemon

6 ripe pears
1 lemon

To Make Sugar Syrup:
In a clean pot, place warm water, adding the sugar and juice of 1 lemon. Bring the sugar syrup to a gentle simmer while preparing the pears.

Poaching the Pears:
Prepare the pears by decoring through the bottom with a small melon baller dipped in lemon juice. Leave the stem intact. Trim off the bottom of the pear to ensure upright stability. Peel the pears, rubbing with lemon to prevent oxidation or browning. Place prepared pears into the sugar syrup and poach without returning to a simmer. Turn the pears after a couple of minutes to cook the other side. Test pears with skewer until done. Remove to a flat-bottomed pan and refrigerate.

Zabaglione:
8 egg yolks
¾ cup sugar
Pinch salt
¼ teaspoon vanilla

½ cup dry Vermouth
1 cup Grand Marnier (orange liqueur)

For best results, use a thick enameled cast-iron pan. Mix the egg yolks, sugar, salt and vanilla together. Whisk until a heavy ribbon is formed. Place over medium flame and add the Vermouth in small amounts to keep a light silky texture. After Vermouth is all in, repeat with Grand Marnier. With all the liqueur in at silky texture, remove and serve over pears. Garnish with toasted pignolls.

Garnish:
¾ cup pignoli nuts

Butter

Sauté pignoli nuts in butter until golden. Strain through a colander and allow the nuts to hang for a couple of minutes to cool.

VEAL ZINGARA
Rusty's, New York City, New York

14 ounces natural leg of veal
2 cups flour
½ onion, diced
1 green pepper, diced
8 fresh mushrooms, sliced
5 ounces pimentos
5 ounces ham, diced
2 pieces artichoke hearts

1 ounce truffles
6 teaspoons beef stock
5 teaspoons red wine
1 teaspoon brandy
Salt to flavor
⅓ teaspoon white pepper
Chopped parsley
Watercress for garnish

Cut veal into small pieces and hammer flat. Cut smaller 2½ ounce pieces and flour both sides. Sauté onion, green pepper and mushrooms in separate pan and remove from pan. Sauté veal pieces in oil and butter in hot pan. When veal is brown on both sides, add onion, green pepper and mushrooms that have already been sauteed. Add pimentos, ham, artichoke hearts and truffles and sauté for 2 minutes. Add beef stock, wine and brandy. Sprinkle lightly with salt and pepper. Garnish with chopped parsley and watercress. Serves 2.

TABLE OF EQUIVALENTS

1 tablespoon = 3 teaspoons
¼ cup = 4 tablespoons
⅓ cup = 5⅓ tablespoons
½ cup = 8 tablespoons
⅔ cup = 10⅔ tablespoons
¾ cup = 12 tablespoons
1 cup = 16 tablespoons
1 liquid ounce = 2 tablespoons
½ pint = 1 cup
1 pint = 2 cups
1 quart = 4 cups
1 gallon = 4 quarts
1 peck = 8 quarts
1 ounce = 2 tablespoons
1 pound almonds in shell = 1½ cups nutmeats
1 pound almonds, shelled = 3 cups chopped
1 pound bananas = 3 medium
1 pound bananas, mashed = 1⅓ cups
1 slice bread with crust = ½ cup soft crumbs
1 8-ounce package dried bread crumbs = 2¼ cups
1 pound butter or margarine = 2 cups or 4 sticks
1 stick butter or margarine = ½ cup or ¼ pound
1 medium bunch of celery = about 4 cups, diced
1 pound Cheddar cheese = 4 cups shredded
¼ pound Swiss or American cheese = 1 cup shredded
1 pound cottage cheese = 2 cups
3 ounces cream cheese = 6 tablespoons
1 pound = 3 cups corn meal
1 square chocolate = 1 ounce = 3 tablespoons cocoa plus 1 tablespoon butter
1 cup whipping cream = 2 cups, whipped
8 ounces sour cream = 1 cup
1 cup egg whites = 8-10 white, large
1 cup egg yolks = 12-14 yolks, large
1 pound all-purpose flour = 4 cups, sifted
1 pound cake flour = 4¾ cups
1 cup cake flour = 1 cup less 2 tablespoons all-purpose flour
1 cup = 9 finely-crumbled salted crackers
1 cup = 11 finely-crumbled graham crackers
1 cup = 30 finely-crumbled vanilla wafers
16 ounces strained honey = 1¼ cups
1 medium lemon = 3 tablespoons = 1 tablespoon grated peel
12 ounces molasses = 2½ cups
1 medium onion = ¾ to 1 cup, chopped

Index

A
All-Bran Muffins, 34
Amazing Coconut Pie, 118
Angel Cheesecake Pie, 116
Apple Bars, 146
" Bread, 143
" Bread, Elaine's, 144
" Bread, Dutch, 144
" Cake, Fresh, 140
" Cake, Iva Lane's, 140
" Cake, Nobby, 141
" Cheese Crunch, 145
" Clafoute, 181
" Crêpes, Broiled, 145
" Crisp, 146
" Crisp, Fresh, 147
" Maple Pudding, 166
" Pie, Cosmopolitan, 142
" Streusel, 142
" Walnut Goodies, 122
Applesauce Nut Bread, 38
" Puffs, 142
Apricot Cream Cheese Delight, 25
Arni Kapama, 171
Artichoke Casserole, 61
" with Yogurt Herb Dip, 161
Asparagus Soup, Toula's Cream of, 20
Au Sable Baked Beans, 44
Aunt Jennie's Refrigerator Cookies, 123
" Mary's Baked Chicken, 59

B
Baked Chicken Breasts Supreme, 58
" Pork Chops with Apples, 80
" Rice Pudding, 137
" Shrimp and Scallops, 55
Banana Bread, 39
" Cream Pie, Coconut, 117
" Loaf, 38
" Oatmeal Drop Cookies, 128
" Split Dessert, 132
Barbara's Barbecued Spareribs, 73
Barbecued Beef on Buns, 30
" Sauce, 79
" Spareribs, 73
Basic Cream Pie Filling and Variations, 115
" Crêpes, 101
Bavarian Pot Roast, 75
Beans, Au Sable Baked, 44
BEEF:
  Barbara's Barbecued Spareribs, 73
  Barbecued Beef on Buns, 30
  Barbecued Spareribs, 73
  Bavarian Pot Roast, 75
  Beef Broccoli, 162
  Beef Burgundy, 76
  Beef over Rice, Tomato, 76
  Beef Stew, 21
  Flank Steak Pinwheels, 74
  Italian Breaded Steak, 74
  Italian Pot Roast, 75
  London Broil Lord Essex, 164
  Pepper Steak, 92
  Prime London Broil, 170
  Reuben Bake, 77
  Corned Beef Rolls, 11
  Shish Kabob, 163
  Beef Teriyaki, 158
  Tosi's Bistecca al Pepe Nero, 170
BEEF, GROUND:
  Casserole Napoli, 95
  Porcupine Balls, 72
  Stuffed Cabbage Rolls, 163
Beets and Eggs, Pickled, 16
Beer Bread, 33
Berta Potatoes, 49
Blender-Oven Catsup, 78
Blueberry Bread, 149
" Bundt Cake, 148
" Cake, 148
" Muffins, 149
" Pie, 147
Blue Cheese Dressing, 28
Bourbon Cocktail Hot Dogs, 12
BREADS:
  Apple, 143
  Applesauce Nut, 38
  Banana, 39
  Beer, 33
  Blueberry, 149
  Brown, 32
  Carrot-Pineapple, 40
  Cranberry Nut, 153
  Dutch Apple, 144
  Elaine's Apple, 144
  Grandma's Bread, 32
  Grandma's White, 33
  Paschaline Psomi, 98
  Pumpkin Nut, 40
  Raisin Nut, 41
  Rhubarb, 41
  Squash, 179
  Zucchini Squash, 42
Broiled Apple Crêpes, 145
Broccoli Beef, 162
" Casserole, Festive, 160
" Cheese-Rice Casserole, 45
" Twenty-Four Hour, 16
Brown Bread, 32
Brownies, 121
Buns, Hamburger, 37
Burger, Crab, 30
Busy Day Chicken, 59
Butter Cream Frosting, 114
Butterscotch Torte, 133

C
Cabbage Rolls, 45
" Rolls, Stuffed, 163
Cake, Blueberry, 148
" Blueberry Bundt, 148
" Carrot, 111

185

Index

" Cherry Chocolate, 151
" Cherry-Pineapple, 150
" Chocolate, 103
" Chocolate Pudding, 103
" Chocolate Sheath, and Frosting, 102
" Cookie Sheet, 110
" Christmas Angel, 155
" Cranberry Sauce, 153
" Dream, 105
" Eclair, 106
" Fourteen Karat, 105
" Fresh Apple, 140
" Grandma, 107
" Granny, 112
" Iva Lane's Apple, 140
" Jiffy Pineapple Dream, 109
" Lemon Cheese, 104
" Nobby Apple, 141
" Pineapple, 111
" Pink Cloud, 156
" Poppy Seed, 108
" Potato, 109
" Pumpkin Pie, 113
" Red Velvet, 115
" Spice Bundt, 110
" Texas Sheet, 113
" Tillie's French Pastry, 106
" Tomato Soup, 112
" Travelin', 141
" Wacky, 104
" with Butter Sauce, Juicy Pineapple, 108
California Style Italian Spaghetti Sauce and Meat Balls, 71
CANDY:
  Mocha Pecan Fudge, 136
  Peanut Cho-Co Nut Fudge, 165
Carolina Cole Slaw, 21
Carrots and Vegetables, Crisp Marinated, 17
" Cake, 111
" Casserole, 46
" Marinated, 18
" Pineapple Bread, 40
" Relish, 16
" Supreme, 17
CASSEROLES:
  Artichoke, 61
  Broccoli-Cheese Rice, 45
  Carrot, 46
  Chicken, 60
  Chop Suey, 89
  Festive Broccoli, 60
  Green Bean, 47
  Good-bye Turkey, 64
  Macaroni, 67
  Napoli, 95
  of Celery, 46
  Pizza, 69
  Shrimp and Cheese, 54
  Vegetable, 51

Catsup, Blender-Oven, 78
Celery, Casserole of, 46
" Exotic, 46
" Seed Dressing, 28
Charley's Chowder, 177
Cheese Bake, Party, 8
" Casserole, Shrimp and, 54
" Casserole, Zucchini and, 52
" Croquettes, 67
" Delights, 9
" Rice Casserole, Broccoli, 45
" Rarebit, 68
" Soufflé, 173
Cherry Chews, 150
" Chocolate Cake, 151
" Pineapple Cake, 150
" Pineapple Salad, 26
Chewy Noels, 130
CHICKEN:
  Aunt Mary's Baked Chicken, 59
  Baked Chicken Breasts Supreme, 58
  Busy Day Chicken, 59
  Chicken and Rice, 61
  Chicken Casserole, 60
  Chicken Delmar, 171
  Chicken Divine, 59
  Chicken Fricassee, 85
  Chicken Gabrielle, 172
  Chicken Kiev, 161
  Chicken Tacos, 87
  Delicious Chicken for Timbales, 63
  Easy Chicken and Rice, 62
  Easy Honey Curried Baked Chicken, 62
  Hot Chicken Salad, 62
  Hot Delicious Chicken Salad, 63
  Le Poulet Au Vinaigre, 172
  Maria's Way Chicken Breasts, 60
  Mulligatawney Soup, 176
  Peanut Chicken, 173
  Teriyaki Chicken, 172
Chili Sauce, Indian, 79
Chilies Rellenos, 95
Chinese Egg Rolls, 90
Chocolate Cake, 103
" Ice Box Dessert, 138
" Mousse, 181
" Pie, 117
" Pudding Cake, 103
" Sheath Cake and Frosting, 102
" Strata Pie, 180
Chop Suey, 89
" Casserole, 89
Christmas Angel Cake, 155
Church Windows, 121
Cobbler, Southern, 154
Coconut or Banana Cream Pie, 117
" Pie, E-Z, 118
Cocktail Meatballs, 10
Concord Grape Pie, 155

Index

COOKIES:
  Apple Bars, 146
  Apple Walnut Goodies, 122
  Aunt Jennie's Refrigerator Cookies, 123
  Banana Oatmeal Drop, 128
  Chewy Noels, 130
  Date Drop Cookies, 124
  Diabetic Sugarless Orange Cookies, 130
  Festive Mint Bars, 127
  Hermit Oatmeal, 127
  Holiday Fruit Cookies, 125
  Holiday Fruit Drops, 124
  Krusties, 129
  Lemon Bars, 126
  Lemon Squares, 125
  Maple Nut Cookies, 122
  O. Henry Bars, 128
  Oatmeal Crispies, 128
  Oatmeal-Jam Bars, 129
  Perfect Raisin Cookies, 131
  Potato Chip Cookies, 130
  Pumpkin Squares, 131
  Sheet Cake, 110
  Stuffed Date Drops, 123
Corned Beef Rolls, 11
Cosmopolitan Apple Pie, 142
Crab Burger, 30
  "   Spread, 158
  "   Supreme, 56
Crabmeat and Mushroom Casserole, 57
Cranberry Mousse with Raspberry Sauce, 154
  "   Nut Bread, 153
  "   Salad, Julie's Frozen, 152
  "   Sauce Cake, 153
Crazy Crust Pie, 68
Cream Cheese Delight, Apricot, 25
Crêpes, Broiled Apple, 145
Crescent Refrigerator Rolls, 34
Crisp Marinated Carrots and Vegetables, 17
Croquettes, Cheese, 67
Crystallized Orange Nuts, 165
Cucumbers Au Gratin, 47

D
Danish Kringle, 96
  "   Pastry, 132
Date Drop Cookies, 124
Delicious Chicken for Timbales, 63
  "   Hot Chicken Salad, 63
  "   Pie, 119
  "   Spaghetti Pie, 70
DESSERT:
  Apple Cheese Crunch, 145
  Apple Clafoute, 181
  Apple Crisp, 146
  Applesauce Puffs, 142
  Apple Streusel, 142
  Baked Rice Pudding, 137
  Banana Split Dessert, 132
  Butterscotch Torte, 133
  Cherry Chews, 150
  Chocolate Ice Box Dessert, 138
  Danish Pastry, 132
  Dutch Apple Delight, 143
  Four Layer, 135
  Fresh Apple Crisp, 147
  Hot Fudge Sauce, 135
  Lemon Dessert, 136
  My Favorite Cobbler, 151
  Pistachio Dessert, 134
  Poached Pears with Grand Marnier Zabaglione, 182
  Quick Peach Crumble, 166
  Rhubarb Crunch, 134
  Taylor Duff, 137
Diabetic Sugarless Orange Cookies, 130
Dip, Artichokes with Yogurt Herb, 161
  "   Easy Hot Sea, 160
  "   Fresh Vegetable, 13
  "   Raw Vegetable, 12
  "   Vegetable, 13
Dream Cake, 105
Dressing, Blue Cheese, 28
  "   Celery Seed, 28
  "   Easy Caesar Salad, 29
Dutch Apple Bread, 144
  "   Apple Delight, 143

E
E-Z Coconut Pie, 118
Easy Caesar Salad Dressing, 29
  "   Chicken and Rice, 62
  "   Honey Curried Baked Chicken, 62
  "   Hot Sea Dip, 160
Eclair Cake, 106
Egg Foo Yung, 88
Eggs, Pickled Beets and, 16
Eggplant, Stuffed, 162
Elaine's Apple Bread, 144
Exotic Celery, 46

F
Festive Broccoli Casserole, 160
  "   Mint Bars, 127
Finnish Sweet Rolls, 97
FISH:
  Baked Fish Soufflé, 57
  Inn's Brook Trout, 175
  Shrimp and Crab Stuffed Flounder, 174
  Stuffed Red Snapper with Shrimp, 175
Flank Steak Pinwheels, 74
Flossie's Company Pork Chops, 80
Foolproof Pie Crust, 115
Four Layer Dessert, 135
Fourteen Karat Cake, 105
French Chocolate Pie, 179
  "   Salad Dressing, 29
  "   Silk Pie, 116
Fresh Apple Cake, 140
  "   Apple Crisp, 147
  "   Vegetable Dip, 13
Frosting, Butter Cream, 114

Index

Frozen Cranberry Salad, 152
" Pumpkin Pie, 119
" Salad, 26
Fruit Magic, 100
Fudge Cream Bars, 100

G
Gala Pecan Spread, 14
German Potato Salad, 22
" Potato Salad, 178
Gelatin Magic, 102
Gingerbread, Sunday Best, 123
Good-bye Turkey Casserole, 64
Gothka Rolls, 36
Grandma's Bread, 32
Grandma's Cake, 107
Grandma's White Bread, 33
Gramma's, Breakfast Popovers, 35
Granny Cake, 112
Green Beans, 48
" Bean Casserole, 47
" Tomato Mincemeat, 18
Grilled Leg of Lamb, 77
Guacamole with Winter Vegetables, 13

H
Ham and Potato Skillet, 78
Hamburger Buns, 37
" Pie, 72
Hawaiian Dessert, 101
Hermit Oatmeal Cookies, 126
Hillbilly Cake, 107
Holiday Appetizer Pie, 12
" Fruit Cookies, 125
" Fruit Drops, 124
" Meatballs, 10
Hot Chicken Salad, 62
" Crabmeat Spread, 15
" Dogs, Bourbon Cocktail, 12
" Fudge Sauce, 135
" Potato Salad, 22

I
Impossible Pie, 100
Indian Chili Sauce, 78
Inn's Brook Trout, 175
Italian Breaded Steak, 74
" Garden Soup, 20
" Pot Roast, 75
Iva Lane's Apple Cake, 140

J
Jello, Rhubarb/Strawberry, 27
Jiffy Pineapple Dream Cake, 109
Joe Muer's Bean Relish, 178
Juicy Pineapple Cake with Butter Sauce, 108
Julie's Frozen Cranberry Salad, 152

K
Kibbi, 84
Krustie, 129

L
LAMB:
  Arni Kapama, 171
  Grilled Leg of Lamb, 77

Kibbi, 84
Lasagne, 94
Layered Green Salad, 24
Lemon Bars, 126
" Cheese Cake, 104
" Dessert, 136
" Squares, 125
Le Poulet Au Vinaigre, 172
Liver Paste, 14
London Broil Lord Essex, 164

M
Macaroni Casserole, 67
Magic Meatballs, 11
Maple Nut Cookies, 122
Marinated Carrots, 18
Meatballs, Cocktail, 10
" Holiday, 10
" Magic, 11
" Mother Revzin's, 9
Medley Casserole, Vegetable, 51
" Vegetable, 50
Mincemeat, Green Tomato, 18
Minestrone, 21
Mint Bars, Festive, 127
Mocha Pecan Fudge, 136
Mother Revzin's Meatballs, 9
Mousse, Chocolate, 181
" Cranberry with Raspberry Sauce, 154
Muffins, All-Bran, 34
" Blueberry, 149
" Sandwiches, 29
Mushroom Casserole, Crabmeat and, 57
My Favorite Cobbler, 151

N
Nobby Apple Cake, 141

O
O. Henry Bars, 128
Oatmeal Crispies Cookies, 128
" Jam Bars, 129
Old Fashion Cream of Tomato Soup, 177
Onion Pie, 48
Oysters and Corn, Scalloped, 176
" Rockefeller, 54
" Scalloped, 55

P
Party Cheese Bake, 8
Paste, Liver, 14
Paschaline Psomi, 98
Paté, Peanut Butter, 14
Peanut Brittle, 166
" Butter Paté, 14
" Butter Pie, 118
" Cho-Co Nut Fudge, 165
" Chicken, 173
Pepper Steak, 92
Perfect Raisin Cookies, 131
Pickled Beets and Eggs, 16
Pickles, Pizza, 8

188

Index

PIES:
   Amazing Coconut Pie, 119
   Angel Cheesecake Pie, 116
   Blueberry, 147
   Chocolate, 117
   Chocolate Strata, 180
   Coconut or Banana Cream, 117
   Concord Grape, 115
   Cosmopolitan Apple, 142
   Crazy Crust Pie, 68
   Delicious Pie, 119
   E-Z Coconut, 118
   French Chocolate, 179
   French Silk Pie, 116
   Frozen Pumpkin, 119
   Hamburger Pie, 72
   Holiday Appetizer, 12
   Impossible Pie, 100
   Onion, 48
   Peanut Butter, 118
   Pineapple Angel, 119
   Pumpkin, 120
   Pumpkin Chiffon, 120
   Spaghetti, 69
   Wine, 179
Pie Crust, Foolproof, 115
   " Filling and Variations, Basic Cream, 115
Pineapple Angel Pie, 119
   " Bread, Carrot, 40
   " Cake, 111
   " Poppins, 39
   " Salad, Cherry, 26
Pink Cloud Cake, 156
Pistachio Dessert, 134
Pizza Casserole, 69
Pizza Pickles, 8
Poached Pears with Grand Marnier Zabaglione, 182
Popcorn Wreath, 165
Popovers, Gramma's Breakfast, 35
Poppins, Pineapple, 39
Poppy Seed Cake, 108
Porcupine Balls, 72
PORK:
   Baked Pork Chops with Apples, 80
   Flossie's Company Pork Chops, 80
   Pork Roast with Sweet and Sour Sauce, 168
   Roast "Pig" Hawaiian, 164
   The Embers Pork Chops, 169
Potatoes Au Gratin, 160
   " Berta, 49
   " Cake, 109
   " Chip Cookies, 130
   " Goodie, 48
Prime London Broil, 170
Pudding, Apple Maple, 166
   " Baked Rice, 137
Pumpkin Chiffon Pie, 120
   " Nut Bread, 40
   " Pie, 120
   " Pie Cake, 113
   " Pie Frozen, 119
   " Squares, 131

Q
Quiche, Spinach, 66
Quiche, Sunday Brunch, 66
Quick Peach Crumble, 166

R
Raisin Nut Bread, 41
Raw Vegetable Dip, 12
Red Velvet Cake, 115
Refrigerator Rolls, 36
Relish, Carrot, 16
Reuben Bake, 77
Rhubarb Bread, 41
   " Crunch, 134
   " Strawberry Jello, 27
Ribbon Salad, 27
Rice Casserole, Broccoli-Cheese, 45
   " Oriental, 92
Roast, Bavarian Pot, 75
   " Italian Pot, 75
   " Pig Hawaiian, 164
Rockefeller, Oysters, 54
Rolls, Cabbage, 45
   " Crescent Refrigerator, 34
   " Finnish Sweet, 97
   " Gothka, 36
   " Refrigerator, 36
   " Yellow. 35

S
SALAD:
   Cherry-Pineapple, 26
   Delicious Hot Chicken, 63
   Dressing, French, 29
   Frozen Salad, 26
   Frozen Cranberry, 152
   German Potato, 178
   German Potato, 22
   Hot Chicken Salad, 62
   Hot Potato, 22
   Julie's Frozen Cranberry Salad, 152
   Layered Green Salad, 24
   Ribbon Salad, 27
   Spinach Salad, 23
   Spinach Salad with Dressing, 24
   Strawberry Salad, 28
   Tomato Shrimp, 23
   Twenty Four Hour Salad, 25
Salmon or Trout, Smoked, 58
Sandwiches, Muffin, 29
Saturday Special, 70
Saucy Sauces for Vegetables, 159
Sausage Soufflé, 79
Scallops, Baked Shrimp and, 55
   " Oysters, 55
   " Oysters and Corn, 176
Shellfish Sorrento, 56

Index

Shish Kabob, 163
Shrimp and Cheese Casserole, 54
" and Crab Stuffed Flounder, 174
" and Scallops, Baked, 55
" Mushroom, 93
" Salad, Tomato, 23
" Spread, 15
Slaw, Carolina Cole, 21
" Twenty-Four Hour Cabbage, 22
Smoked Salmon or Trout, 58
Sorrento, Shellfish, 56
Soufflé Baked Fish, 57
" Cheese, 173
SOUP:
   Charley's Chowder, 177
   Chicken Mulligatawney, 176
   Italian Garden Soup, 20
   Old Fashion Cream of Tomato, 177
   Toula's Cream of Asparagus, 20
Southern Cobbler, 154
Spaghetti Pie, 69
" Pie, Delicious, 70
" Sauce with Meatballs, California Style Italian, 71
Spareribs, Barbara's Barbecued, 73
" Barbecued, 73
Spice Bundt Cake, 111
Spinach Quiche, 66
" Salad, 23
" Salad with Dressing, 24
Spread, Gala Pecan, 14
" Hot Crabmeat, 15
" Shrimp, 15
" Super Great Crab, 15
Squash Bread, 179
" Bread, Zucchini, 42
" Casserole, Summer, 49
Steak, Italian Breaded, 74
" Pepper, 92
" Pinwheels Flank, 74
Stew, Beef, 21
Stewed Tomato Casserole, 50
Strawberry Jello, Rhubarb, 27
" Salad, 28
Stuffed Cabbage Rolls, 163
" Date Drops, 123
" Eggplant, 162
" Red Snapper with Shrimp, 175
Summer Squash Casserole, 49
Sunday Best Gingerbread, 121
" Brunch Quiche, 66
Super Great Crab Spread, 15
Swedish Christmas Sausage, 86

T

Tacos, Chicken, 87
Taylor Duff, 137
Teriyaki Chicken, 172
Texas Sheet Cake, 113
The Embers' Pork Chops, 169
Tillie's French Pastry Cake, 106

Tomato Casserole, Stewed, 50
" Beef Over Rice, 76
" Shrimp Salad, 23
" Soup Cake, 112
Tosi's Bistecca al Pepe Nero, 170
Toula's Cream of Asparagus Soup, 20
Travelin' Cake, 141
Trout, Smoked Salmon or, 58
Turkey Casserole, Good-bye, 64
" "The Inside Story", 64
Twenty Four Hour Broccoli, 16
" Cabbage Slaw, 22
" Salad, 25

V

Veal Scallopine, 168
" Zingara, 183
Vegetable Casserole, 51
" Dip, 13
" Guacamole with Winter, 13
" Medley, 50
" Medley Casserole, 51

W

Wacky Cake, 104
Wine Pie, 179

Y

Yams, Yummy, 52
Yellow Rolls, 35
Yugoslav Kifle, 96
Yummy Yams, 52

Z

Zabaglione, 91
Zucchini and Cheese Casserole, 52
" San Lu Rae, 93
" Squash Bread, 42
Zuppa Stracciatella Con Spinaci, 85

Re-Order Additional Copies

American Cancer Society
Michigan Division, Inc.
1205 E. Saginaw
Lansing, Michigan 48906

Please send _____ copies of MICHIGAN COOKS' COLLECTION at $5.00 per copy (plus $.85 per copy for postage and handling)

I enclose an additional donation of $_____.

Enclosed is my check or money order for $_____
(make checks payable to the American Cancer Society.)

Name _____

Address _____

City _____ County _____ State _____ Zip _____

American Cancer Society
Michigan Division, Inc.
1205 E. Saginaw
Lansing, Michigan 48906

Please send _____ copies of MICHIGAN COOKS' COLLECTION at $5.00 per copy (plus $.85 per copy for postage and handling)

I enclose an additional donation of $_____.

Enclosed is my check or money order for $_____
(make checks payable to the American Cancer Society.)

Name _____

Address _____

City _____ County _____ State _____ Zip _____

American Cancer Society
Michigan Division, Inc.
1205 E. Saginaw
Lansing, Michigan 48906

Please send _____ copies of MICHIGAN COOKS' COLLECTION at $5.00 per copy (plus $.85 per copy for postage and handling)

I enclose an additional donation of $_____.

Enclosed is my check or money order for $_____
(make checks payable to the American Cancer Society.)

Name _____

Address _____

City _____ County _____ State _____ Zip _____